"This book is both timely and helpf albeit well-researched, perspective i ality in the concept of existence's ongoing developmental manifestation of a deeper underlying wholeness. He offers a compelling argument that such a holistic shift in human perspective will . . . help ensure our survival and ongoing evolution in consciousness as a species. This commendable effort is to be welcomed with gratitude."

—CLAUDIUS VAN WYK
Co-convenor, the Holos Earth Project

"We simply *must* find a way forward beyond outdated and provincial religious constructs . . . . Yet, the human spirit still cries out for a way to connect with something greater than the self! Olson's inspired portrayal of consciousness provides a cutting-edge approach to spiritual meaning and fulfillment in our increasingly post-religious world. Further, the groundbreaking applications he describes have the power to spur a very much needed societal transformation."

—MARGARET PLACENTRA JOHNSTON
author of *Faith Beyond Belief: Stories of Good People Who Left Their Church Behind*

"What I loved most about this book is how accessible it is. There is a simplicity and an honesty and a true humanity coming through the author that makes reading it a warm and wholesome, very pleasant, and heart-opening experience. . . . The author manifests in his writings not just the concepts but the inner feeling tone of exactly what the wholeness is that he is talking about."

—SHOSHANA COOPER
Meditation Teacher

"I am ever thankful for *Become Conscious of Wholeness* and see it as an invaluable resource for our world today! . . . The wholeness that Ed speaks about brings us face to face with our true self beyond senses, mind, and intellect. Ed's book breaks down these complex concepts of science and spirituality with candor and grace and propels them into mainstream reality."

—JOANNE WOHLMUTH
Yoga Teacher/Yoga Therapist

"*Become Conscious of Wholeness* deserves your full attention. Well-researched and clearly thought-out, it argues that the experience and personal integration of universal consciousness is the only real solution to humanity's rapidly accelerating existential climate crisis. . . . Imbibe deeply from this book. Let it change you and the world."

—JOHN ROBINSON
author of *Aging with Vision, Hope and Courage in a Time of Crisis*

"Olson has summarized well that the only future open for humans is to find a common basis in consciousness or conscious spirit of which we are all a part . . . . I hope the book reaches many people. We humans are undergoing a tremendous transition, and people need to be reminded of who they really are and their connection to the Source. Only this way can we all do what we have come here to do!"

—TINA LINDHARD
Chair of Consciousness Research, CICA International

"Edwin Olson is a voice of clarity and authenticity in this current chaotic moment in human history. His book is an invitation to reimagine how humanity might experience itself in loving connection with its Source. . . . Olson's gentle scholarship weaves quantum science, theology, mysticism, and depth psychology into a new story, one in which the divine and humanity's place in the cosmos are exquisitely reconsidered. . . . This is a book for our time."

—MARY HARRELL
author of *The Mythmaker*

Become Conscious of Wholeness

2/9/22

For Lerita,

In anticipation of learning from you at Blowing Rock,

Ed

PREVIOUS BOOKS BY EDWIN E. OLSON

Facilitating Organization Change: Lessons from Complexity Science.
San Francisco: Jossey-Bass/Wiley, 2001.

Keep the Bathwater: Emergence of the Sacred in Science and Religion.
Estero, FL: Island Sound, 2009. Available from author.

Finding Reality: Four Ways of Knowing.
Bloomington, IN: Archway, 2014.

And God Created Wholeness: A Spirituality of Catholicity.
Maryknoll, NY: Orbis, 2018. (Received the First Place Award in Faith and Science in 2019 by the Catholic Press Association in the United States and Canada.)

Become Conscious of Wholeness

Humanity's Only Future

EDWIN E. OLSON

Foreword by Ilia Delio

Illustrations by Tuesday Hadden

RESOURCE *Publications* · Eugene, Oregon

BECOME CONSCIOUS OF WHOLENESS
Humanity's Only Future

Resource Publications
An Imprint of Wipf and Stock Publishers
199 W. 8th Ave., Suite 3
Eugene, OR 97401

www.wipfandstock.com

PAPERBACK ISBN: 978-1-6667-3120-0
HARDCOVER ISBN: 978-1-6667-2343-4
EBOOK ISBN: 978-1-6667-2345-8

.   NOVEMBER 17, 2021 8:42 AM

To my family[1]:

James, Lynn Patricia, Arne, and Greta Olson

Eric, Dinah, Arlo, and Zeida Olson

Loren, Lynn Maria, and Preston Olson

Amy, Shane, Tuesday, Cisco, and Clover Hadden

And the best

Wife, Mom, and Grandma

Who continues to inspire and sustain us all,

Judith

---

1. See *Appendix A: My Extended Family.*

Contents

LIST OF ILLUSTRATIONS

Foreword

Ilia Delio, OSF

IN HER BRILLIANT ESSAY ON space and transcendence, Margaret Wertheim claimed that we have become lost in space and are undergoing a spiritual crisis of Newtonian cosmology.[1] We severed our relationship with nature about five hundred years ago when the philosopher René Descartes declared that the mind is separate and distinct from matter: *Cogito ergo sum.* Descartes' dualism provided the basis for disregarding the earth and all creaturely life; it also paved the way for modern science to develop without interference from religion. Cartesian philosophy basically stated that matter is inert stuff, and the human mind is not part of nature. Upon these basic ideas we constructed the disconnected modern world. The Jesuit scientist, Pierre Teilhard de Chardin, indicated that the artificial separation between humans and cosmos is at the root of our contemporary moral confusion. We must either become aware of our radical disconnect from earth or perish in the desert of our destructive choices.

The early twentieth-century discovery of quantum physics was a radical breakthrough for both science and philosophy. For the first time since Descartes, we realized the essential role of the mind in the determination of matter. Quantum physics opened up discussions on mind and matter in a new way, giving rise to the concept of wholistic nature through the discovery of wave-particle duality and the essential role of consciousness. In the same era, the study of biological life yielded to the concept of systems and complex dynamical wholes. Life was seen not as a collection of structures but networks of relationships, where information flowed between interacting systems, giving rise to more complex systems. The notion of systems

1. Wertheim, "Lost in Space: The Spiritual Crisis of Newtonian Cosmology."

existing within systems led to the description of a *holon*, something that is simultaneously a whole and part.[2] Biological life, therefore, began to reveal itself as wholes within wholes of complexifying systems.

Quantum physics, in particular, brought holism to new light by identifying the observer as part of the system, pointing to a fundamental role of consciousness in material reality. David Bohm and Karl Pribam each speculated on wholeness in nature and developed theories to explain wholeness as a function of consciousness. Bohm said there are two ways of seeing the universe. The first is the mechanistic order, in which the universe is seen as a collection of entities existing independently in time and space, and interacting through forces that do not cause any change in the essential nature of these entities. This is the Newtonian perspective, following fundamental laws of classical physics, in which each atom, molecule, cell, organism, or entity acts according to classical physical laws of motion.

The second perspective is based on quantum reality, which cannot be accounted for by the mechanistic order. In quantum reality, movement is generally seen as discontinuous. Particles, like electrons, can show different properties depending on their environment: in some places they are particles while in other places they are waves. Finally, two particles can show "non-local relationships," which means they can be separated by vast distances but react as if they are connected to each other.[3] Bohm recognized that these new features of quantum theory require that the entire universe be considered as an unbroken whole, with each element in that whole demonstrating properties that depend on the overall environment. He put forth these ideas in his book, *Wholeness and Implicate Order*, where he wrote: "Thus, if all actions are in the form of discrete quanta, the interactions between the different entities (e.g., electrons) constitute a single structure of indivisible links, so that the entire universe has to be thought of as an unbroken whole."[4]

Bohm's notion of implicate and explicate orders emphasizes the primacy of structure and process over individual objects. He applied his idea of implicate order to the structure of the universe and to consciousness. He showed that what we usually think of as empty space is full of background

2. For a discussion of holons, see Cannato, *Radical Amazement*; Cannato, *Fields of Compassion: How the New Cosmology is Transforming Spiritual Life*; Wilber, *A Theory of Everything*.

3. Bohm, *Wholeness and Implicate Order*, 175.

4. Bohm, *Wholeness and Implicate Order*, 175.

energy. This immense background energy, he wrote, may be the basis of implicate order and the undivided wholeness of the universe. He provides a clear account of how a "particle" conception of matter not only causes harm to the sciences, but also to the way we think and live, and thus to our very society and its future evolution. He wrote:

> The notion that all these fragments are separately existent is evidently an illusion, and this illusion cannot do other than lead to endless conflict and confusion. Indeed, the attempt to live according to the notion that the fragments are really separate is, in essence, what has led to the growing series of extremely urgent crises that is confronting us today and the creation of an overall environment that is neither physically nor mentally healthy for most of the people who live in it.[5]

The return of mind to matter may be the most significant discovery of our modern age. The physicist Max Planck spoke of consciousness as fundamental to matter; that is, we cannot consider matter apart from consciousness. He wrote:

> All matter originates and exists only by virtue of a force which brings the particle of an atom to vibration and holds this most minute solar system of the atom together. We must assume behind this force the existence of a conscious and intelligent mind. This mind is the matrix of all matter.[6]

Similarly, physicist Erwin Schrödinger thought that consciousness is absolutely fundamental to matter and always experienced in the singular; everything begins with consciousness which itself is immaterial.[7] Sir Arthur Eddington spoke of universal unity—that is, coherence—and suggested that the universe as a coherent system is the basis of the unity of the mind. In his view, "the stuff of the world is mind-stuff."[8] Menas Kafatos and Robert Nadeau have argued that, if the universe is an indivisible wholeness, everything comes out of this wholeness and everything belongs to it, including our own consciousness; thus, consciousness is a cosmic property.[9] Diogo Ponte and Lothar Schäfer suggest that the evolution of life may "no

5. Bohm, *Wholeness and Implicate Order*, 1–2.

6. Borowski, "Quantum Mechanics and the Consciousness Connection."

7. Schrodinger, *What is Life?*, 93–5.

8. Eddington, *The Nature of the Physical World*, 259.

9. Kafatos and Nadeau, *The Conscious Universe*.

longer be a process of the adaption of species to their environment, but as the adaption of minds to increasingly complex forms that exist in the cosmic potentiality."[10]

The nature of consciousness evades all empirical reductionism because consciousness is intrinsic to reality itself; it is a cosmic phenomenon that renders reductionism obsolete. As Bertrand Russell noted, "we know nothing about the intrinsic quality of physical events except when these are mental events that we directly experience."[11] Consciousness cannot be reduced to a property of matter because it is the fundamental entanglement of matter and experience. Hence, the basis of matter is not material; quantum physics opens up matter to mystery and the realm of the numinous. That is, quantum physics renews a place of mystery in the natural world and invites science and religion into a new integral relationship.

Ed Olson takes up these new insights on mind and matter, and weaves them into a new paradigm of wholeness. The reader is invited into a new way of thinking about matter and spirit that reorders our place in the cosmos, not at the top of the ladder but as part of the cosmic whole. This holistic paradigm is fundamental to our future. We cannot continue with our oversized ecological footprint. We are part of conscious nature and, thus, we are part of cosmic wholeness. Such insight opens the doors to a new understanding of spirituality and science, mysticism and matter, nature and spirit. Olson expounds these relationships in clear and insightful ways. This new book reveals a new world where matter, mind, spirit, and God can find new meaning. We are summoned into this new world—better yet—we must enter into it and embrace holism, if we aspire to life abundant.

Ilia Delio, OSF
Connelly Chair in Theology
Villanova University

10. Ponte and Schäfer, "Carl Gustav Jung, Quantum Physics and the Spiritual Mind: A Mystical Vision of the Twenty-First Century."

11. Russell, "Mind and Matter."

Preface

OUR EXISTENTIAL CRISES

> "If we are to flourish, and even to survive, . . . the consciousness of the dominant segment of humanity must change . . . Wake up and become the change we need. The future of a remarkable species on a precious planet is in your hands."[1]
>
> —ERVIN LASZLO

OUR CURRENT WORLDVIEWS HAVE SPLIT the United States and some other Western democracies into warring tribes that perpetuate social and political inequities and upheavals, and the spread of a global pandemic. If we remain divided, we will face unforeseen catastrophic threats that will be devastating. From the Global Trends Report:

> Shared global challenges—including climate change, disease, financial crises, and technology disruptions—are likely to manifest more frequently and intensely in almost every region and country . . . Those intensifying challenges will collide with a geopolitical structure that will become increasingly fragmented and fragile, as the U.S. competes with China for global leadership while citizens of both democracies and autocracies grow more dissatisfied with their leaders.[2]

Contributing to these existential crises is humanity's influence on the climate and ecosystems. We are now the dominant force that has supplanted forces like solar orbit, volcanism, and natural selection, which controlled evolution for most of the planet's 4.5 billion years. We are in the

---

1. Laszlo, *Reconnecting to the Source*, 201–202.
2. *Global Trends Report*, National Intelligence Council.

Anthropocene, the "new epoch in Earth history in which Homo sapiens are blindly steering the ship."[3]

How can we respond to these crises when we have our hands on the wheel of evolution, but we don't agree on the direction to go? Many are trapped in our national, tribal, conspiratorial, and demographic bubbles and destructive material worldviews, and are unaware of our need to connect to a deeper wisdom.

Our view of reality is too small and limited. As the rulers of the Anthropocene, we have forgotten what the ancients knew—that our physical, material reality we experience daily is entwined with a non-material, cosmic, mystical, flowing energy. Our consciousness about that reality can be elevated by accessing Consciousness that was present as an energy wave at the Big Bang (or whenever time and space began) and has been evolving to the present.

Think of Consciousness as the light of reality that enters the prism of our human consciousness to cast colorful and diverse light to enlighten creation. As such, Consciousness is continually reframing, reimagining, and reforming our experiences of the physical world, including all of our human constructions. We have the agency and freedom to access the deep wisdom of Consciousness and bring our narrow, material worldviews to a unifying vision of life in a post-pandemic world.

PURPOSE OF BOOK

Theologians, mystics, and scientists have increased their inquiry into the mystery of consciousness and the depth that awaits us there. All of the religious and spiritual paths, and now the quantum sciences, point to Something More, another dimension. But they use different language and often are disrespectful or fearful of paths they do not follow. This book seeks to show that the multiple ways of accessing consciousness all point to a fundamental Consciousness—a common basis for understanding the mystical and spiritual world.

Resolving and transcending these differences is imperative if our present generation will begin to transform the Anthropocene. When the light of Consciousness enters human consciousness, deep change is possible.

With a more rapid and radical change in human consciousness, we will realize we are part of a cosmic wholeness in time to meet the challenge

3. Alex, "The Anthropocene's Ancient Origins."

of the next pandemic, food crisis, shift in immigration patterns, etc. A substantial rise in awareness as individuals, groups, organizations, and nation states connect to Consciousness can save our species and the biosphere.

Our individual human consciousness is like a standing wave in the ocean of Consciousness. As we engage with Consciousness, our unique expression flows into the collective, which in turn can develop a global consciousness.

I hope the reader will find this book helpful in explaining, illuminating, and accessing Consciousness that is all around us.

ACKNOWLEDGMENTS

I AM INDEBTED TO THE courageous theologians, religious and spiritual leaders, and scientists who I have personally known who have opened the boundaries between science, religion, and spirituality. They include Rev. Charles Colberg, Rev. Bruce Sanguin, Rev. Walter Fohs (deceased), Rev. Michael Dowd, Karen Woods, Rev. Michael Morwood, Dr. John Crowell, Dr. Charles (Billy) Gunnels, Chet Raymo, Claudius van Wyk, and particularly Dr. Ilia Delio, OSF, who included *And God Created Wholeness: A Spirituality of Catholicity* in her "Catholicity in an Evolving Universe" series for Orbis Books and who has honored me with the Foreword to this book.

I am grateful to the members and friends of Uplands Village, Pleasant Hill, Tennessee, as I developed my understanding of Consciousness and its implications for our lives. Rev. Ron Johnson, Karen Woods, Don Nelson, Rev. Lyle Weible, Rev. Marvin Albright, Rev. Ted McKnight, Gail Ford, Dr. Janeen Carrell, Karen Charbonnet, Deborah Holbrook, Rev. Phil Nevius, Sue Peeples, Linda Persohn, Don Rainer, Dr. James and Gail Swanbeck, Jerry Ziegle, and the Uplands Lifelong Learning Center (ULLI) have been especially helpful.

During the lockdown with COVID-19, I was fortunate to share early drafts of this manuscript with colleagues around the world including Claudius van Wyk (Spain), Dr. Finley Lawson (England), Joanne Wohlmuth (Bermuda), Margaret Placentra Johnston (Virginia), Tom Dunne (Maryland), Nanette Smith (Pennsylvania), Shane Hadden (Kentucky), Judy Charland (Florida), Dr. Eric Olson (New York), Dr. Anita Wood (Ohio), Fr. David Cooper (Wisconsin), and my Tennessee colleagues (Karen Woods, Mary Schantz, Rev. Mark Canfield, Shoshana Cooper, and Rev. Ron Johnson). Their comments helped me navigate the complex scientific, philosophical, and religious terrain of Consciousness.

Kudos to Tuesday Hadden, my granddaughter, for creating the illustrations in the book (https://www.tuesdayhadden.com). I appreciate the careful copyediting, clarifying questions, and insights from Melinda Thiessen Spencer, and the support of Matt Wilmer and his colleagues at Wipf and Stock Publishers.

The impetus for starting this book was Mark Gober's *An End to Upside-down Thinking* and a question posed to me by Karen Woods: "What About Consciousness?"

Ed Olson
Uplands Village, Pleasant Hill, Tennessee
July 26, 2021

Introduction

BECOMING CONSCIOUS OF WHOLENESS

TO DEAL WITH OUR EXISTENTIAL crises, we need to base our disagreements on the same facts, burst out of our bubbles of tribalism, and see our essential unity. We need a blueprint for renewing our individual and collective consciousness, transforming our organizations and institutions, and re-enchanting our societies.

The good news is that we can create a new narrative for our lives that will be inclusive and transform our worldview as we broaden our understanding of truth, beauty, and goodness. Think of Universal Consciousness as fields of flowing energy in which we transform our human consciousness, engage our neighbors, and build a society.

David Bohm described a hidden domain of reality that we take for granted. He referred to the vast star-filled emptiness, the vacuum, the infinity of outer space as a *Plenum*, something that is infinitely full rather than infinitely empty. He saw the emptiness as fullness, as one whole, living organism—an undivided wholeness in flowing movement. I believe this describes the field of Universal Consciousness.

Our interactions, our choices in this field of Consciousness, affect all of nature and life in the biosphere. We can help nature and life to flourish, or we can continue to break down the natural evolution of nature and manifest catastrophes like COVID-19.

Neuroscientists study and map consciousness' connection to the brain. Psychologists explore consciousness as a function of the psyche (mind). Everyone associates consciousness with their awareness of sensations, intuition, and experience.

How we think about the origin of our conscious experience has profound implications for how we think about ourselves and our civilization. If we regard our consciousness as solely generated by ourselves and our environment, we will pursue narrow individual goals for the benefit of the few while the many suffer, including other living creatures and the planet itself.

If we regard our consciousness as being informed by Universal Consciousness, we will be open to the wisdom, intelligence, and love that are essential for us to act for the good of the whole. Without this intelligence, nature does not create and evolve.

REGAINING WISDOM FROM THE "GROUND OF OUR BEING"

For eons, the natural laws of the universe were the dominant forces on our planet as sentient life emerged. When human beings developed self-awareness, they intuited that these forces were goddesses and gods. They were variously named God, Yahweh, Allah, the Absolute, One Mind, Spirit, Advanta, Braham, Tao, Nirvana, and Source, among many other names. All characterizations of a Divine power were human constructions to express insights about the "ground of our being"[1] and provide answers to such existential questions as, "Why do I exist?" and "What does my existence mean?"

As humans developed greater confidence and power to answer these questions for themselves, they began to impose their will on the natural order (regardless of any wisdom from the "ground of our being") through the Renaissance, the Enlightenment, the Industrial Revolution, and atomic power. Nature and all of life are suffering as a result.

When we access Consciousness, we regain that connection, that compassion, that sense of wholeness from "the ground of our being" that has saved our species in the past.

> You think because you understand "one" you must also understand "two,"
> because one and one make two. But you must also understand "and."

> —MAWLANA JALAL-AL-DIN RUMI

---

1. The distinguished theologian Paul Tillich famously suggested that God be understood as the "ground of Being-Itself," the ground upon which all beings exist, in *Systematic Theology*, vol. 1.; Aldous Huxley identified the ground of our being as the Perennial Wisdom, an inherent divine reality we long for, in *The Doors of Perception*.

The "and" in the quote by Rumi is Consciousness. There is one reality, not two.

Consciousness is the single, underlying reality from which the tremendously diverse philosophies and religious and primordial traditions of the world emerged.

Reframing of religion and spirituality through the light from consciousness is a response to Teilhard's insights that "a new story of the cosmos demands a *new understanding of God* (italics added) and a new understanding of ourselves in relation to God."[2]

Responses to our existing crises that arise from accessing Consciousness will be based on our collective spiritual experiences of profound wisdom—the profound wisdom that has been acknowledged for ages but has been eroded by secularization of society. We have tried to fill the void with material accomplishments.

THE NEW SCIENCES

Reductionist science has stripped out what it means to be human—our essential morality and connection to other beings and the planet itself. With the development of quantum theory, there is a possibility of moving to the next stage of evolution where we will encounter several marvels, which are the core characteristics of the conscious universe.[3] Science is reductive as it isolates parts of the whole and controls for complex variables that influence its findings. For a rigorous analysis of a mechanical process, this is vital. However, to comprehend the reality of how we are infinitely connected through Consciousness, a post-material science based on quantum theory is necessary.

This is a worldview that recognizes that consciousness is fundamental in nature, integral to our mental processes—not somehow generated by the firing of neurons in the brain. Wholeness is the symbol of this worldview that will develop the collective knowledge to minimize humanity's environmental impact and steer us to a sustainable future.

2. Delio, *Hours of the Universe*, xvi.
3. Kafatos, Bridging the Perceived Gap.

ORGANIZATION OF BOOK

To ensure the survival of our species and the biosphere, we need to become conscious of our wholeness. Richard Rohr says, "Somehow our occupation and vocation as believers in this sad time must be to connect to Consciousness. What other power do we have now?"[4] This book explicitly shows how to connect to Consciousness, the source of the power we do have.

The book builds on a model of the dimensions of Consciousness I discuss in *And God Created Wholeness*.[5] By moving through the dimensions of Consciousness, readers will confront their own shadow and develop greater personal Wholeness.

Part I. Understanding Consciousness. The energy fields in everything, from atoms to galaxies, and forces like gravity are qualities of the non-material reality, filled with creative potential. Scientists, philosophers, and some theologians now agree with the mystics that this worldview uniquely explains reality.

Chapter 1: Consciousness of Wholeness. Consciousness has been a "Hard Problem" for science to explain without the concepts, methods, or language to measure subjective and mystical phenomena. Now many scientists of quantum physics and quantum biology understand how Consciousness explains their "Eureka" moments.

Chapter 2: What the Brain Does and Does Not. The brain normally filters out from Consciousness only what we need for our survival. When we open the brain's filter through meditation, dreaming, and spiritual practices, and pay attention to what is being sent to the brain from our heart and gut, we access more of Consciousness.

Chapter 3: Universal Consciousness. Consciousness has created everything we experience in the world, the Universe, and the Cosmos—animate and even inanimate. It is the energy in the universe that has usually been named as manifestations of a divine spirit.

Part II. Accessing Universal Consciousness. We have the potential to create a future that is based on a widespread embrace of mysticism, not a return to the illusory past of a material world that led to the COVID-19 pandemic, systemic racism, and other evils.

4. Richard Rohr, "Some Simple But Urgent Guidance To Get Us Through These Next Months," blog, September 19, 2020.

5. Olson, *And God Created Wholeness*. The book received the First Place Award in Faith and Science in 2019 by the Catholic Press Association in the United States and Canada.

Chapter 4: Experiencing the Mystical. To get beyond our material, ego-driven trance about the nature of reality, an intuitive approach is essential.

Chapter 5: Dream Portals to Consciousness. Dreams can be especially useful because they are infinite, transcendent, unbounded, and one with the consciousness of others.

Chapter 6: Waking Portals to Consciousness. Catalysts such as words, symbols, sounds, and stories can open the filter in our brain to access Universal Consciousness.

Chapter 7: Moving Between the Dimensions of Consciousness. Moving through the dimensions of consciousness enables us to become more whole and more spiritual—more fully human.

Part III. Moving Toward Greater Wholeness. Accessing all dimensions of consciousness creates a more holistic Self and society as we individually and collectively confront our "shadows."

Chapter 8: Personal Wholeness. When we encounter our shadow (that part of ourselves that we suppress and sometimes project onto others), we learn to forgive ourselves and bring the shadow into waking consciousness, where its power is transformed into a positive force.

Chapter 9: Collective Wholeness. The collective shadow of racism, sexism, homophobia, and other 'isms keeps us from valuing the deep connection we have with each other, other living species, and the planet itself.

Chapter 10: Becoming an Agent of Holism. We all have the capacity to venture deeply into Consciousness and share that awareness with others.

Part IV. Transforming Our Institutions. Our institutions must use their resources and power to foster the welfare of the biosphere and its inhabitants.

Chapter 11: Reframing Religion. Religion can either be a restraining or motivating force for the personal and collective actions we need. Organized religions can help break the spell of materialism if they revisit their spiritual origins to confront the divisive and consumer-driven forces in society.

Chapter 12: Reimagining Education and Wellness. A non-material worldview can transform our institutions that create and perpetuate our 'isms and materialistic illusions. Our myriad educational and wellness institutions can foster a deeper level of learning.

Chapter 13: Reforming Business and Government. Consciousness can make a significant difference in how business and government respond to a post-pandemic world and take on societal tasks that our political parties have avoided, such as climate change.

Concluding Thoughts: A Compelling Story. Reimagining our reality with Consciousness rewires our priorities to embrace what is of ultimate value—our relationships with each other and the Earth—to create a new global consciousness and ethic.

Shall we look to the past and hope for a return to a fantasized normal? Or should we dig deeper into our collective wisdom and turn the risks of an extended pandemic, food crises, financial crises, climate change, and international conflicts into opportunities?

The current level of our collective consciousness is driving us to a point of no return. The bottom line: we must get out of our boxes and bubbles, and listen to and embrace what Consciousness is trying to tell us through our dreams, intuitions, visions, and images.

Can we develop a collective response to our problems? We can, if we connect to each other in a deep, holistic, and profound way with a world-view that expands and intensifies our vision of a hopeful global future.

Our website Wholeness Consciousness (wholenessconsciousness .com), offers fresh content from diverse perspectives to keep this conversation going. Hopefully, readers will contribute their own ideas for moving us, individually and collectively, toward the Wholeness we need to respond to our existential crises.

Edwin (Ed) Olson, October 26, 2021

Part I

UNDERSTANDING CONSCIOUSNESS

INTRODUCTION: REALITY OF CONSCIOUSNESS

"ONTOLOGY" IS THE ACADEMIC FIELD of *descriptions of reality* that is ultimately based on a belief and faith that what we think we know is true. "Epistemology" is the academic field, based on our senses and intuition, about *how* we know that reality.[1]

Both academic fields struggle to answer these two questions:

1. Did non-material reality have its origins in material reality?

2. Is non-material reality the source of everything, including matter and energy?[2]

In the following chapters we explore these questions. Full disclosure: My ontological belief is that Consciousness, our non-material reality, was the source of everything. I explain how I know this through my own personal inner investigation, which is the only way to answer this question, according to Dr. Tina Lindhard in her review of perspectives about consciousness:

> The fundamental problem of consciousness seems to be related to the question who are we? How we answer this will decide if consciousness is a property of matter, the ground of all existence, or the soul of a timeless conscious Mind or Spirit manifesting itself through matter. It seems that the only way to answer this is

1. Olson, *Finding Reality.*

2. Adapted from Chopra, Is the Afterlife a Non-Question?, 1235–1239 and his Preface in Laszlo, Reconnecting to the Source, xx.

1

through personal inner investigation otherwise we will be relying on what others tell us or on belief.[3]

When I discuss consciousness with a small "*c*," I am referring to the consciousness of any life form, including humans. When I discuss consciousness with a capital "*C*," I am referring to Universal Consciousness.

Chapter 1: Consciousness of Wholeness. We explore our consciousness as awareness of our personhood and our freedom (agency) to make choices. All sentient entities have some degree of self-awareness and freedom. Dog owners are sure their pet is self-aware as it chooses to disobey. All living entities have some limited degree of agency. Raising our consciousness of Wholeness offers our best hope of reducing the negative impact of the Anthropocene and ensuring our survival as a species.

Chapter 2: What the Brain Does and Does Not. We see that the brain, an organ composed of the same kind of atoms and molecules as in the rest of the body, did not become conscious as complex organic chemicals combined. Our consciousness, our freedom (agency), and all the quantum processes of life are connected as well as interconnected to Consciousness—the Cosmic Whole.

Chapter 3: Universal Consciousness. We see the many scientific and philosophic theories and models of the energy fields in the Universe that comprise non-material reality. When we encounter "something more" beyond our everyday experience, it is a moment in time when we are in touch with the non-material reality that is everywhere in the Universe: Consciousness.

3. Lindhard, "Consciousness from the Outside-In and Inside-Out Perspective." Lindhard teaches at the International University of Professional Studies (IUPS) in Hawaii.

Chapter 1

Consciousness of Wholeness

Our consciousness is our means of exploring reality in order to know who we are and what is available to us in the Universe.

And God Created Wholeness[1] contains a model of three dimensions of consciousness that we commonly experience: *Surface, Liminal (Positive and Negative)*, and *Bedrock*, which I called the Wholeness Model. The metaphor of life developed by a quantum biologist and a quantum physicist explains the dimensions:[2]

- Surface: Our waking consciousness of our interactions in the three-dimensional material biosphere.

- Liminal: Our awareness of our turbulent feelings, emotions, energy, and aspirations that motivate the decisions and events in our lives.

- Bedrock: Quantum particles of energy in a continual state of possibility. In psychological terms, this is our dreams and intuitions that link us to Consciousness.

The dimensions are expressions of the essential "withoutness" (outside) and "withinness" (inside) of everything described by Teilhard de Chardin. By the "without" of things, Teilhard refers to physical, tangible,

---

1. Olson, *And God Created Wholeness*. In this book I used the quantum biologist term of "Middle" instead of "Liminal."

2. McFadden and Al-Khalili, *Life on the Edge*. The dimensions also correspond to the three necessary conditions for the existence of consciousness described by a team of a bioscientist, pharmacologist, and psychiatrist in Pereira Jr., et al., *Consciousness and Cosmos: Building an Ontological Framework*, 181–205.

and visible aspects such as size, shape, weight, structure, velocity, and lifespan.[3] This corresponds to the Surface dimension of wholeness.

By the "within" of things, Teilhard refers to their inner actions and events that are intangible and invisible to others. For humans, the "within" is our thoughts, emotions, daydreams, plans, choices, etc.[4] This corresponds to the Liminal dimension of wholeness.

As Teilhard further explains, each cell, each molecule, and each atom has a "within."[5] This corresponds to the Bedrock dimension of quantum interactions that link us to Consciousness.

Following is an explanation of the three dimensions and why they are essential to understanding the evolution of human consciousness. The dimension we most regularly experience is Surface consciousness:

SURFACE CONSCIOUSNESS

In our waking consciousness, we interact with the *biosphere*—the physical, material world of people and things *(Figure 1)*. Surface consciousness comprises the material surface of the earth occupied by living organisms. We experience the fire, air, water, wind, and soil of the earth. It is the macro, everyday world of physical objects, people, nature, and the universe where physical objects and behavior can be observed, measured, and predicted (at least with known probabilities).[6]

3. Savary, *Teilhard de Chardin's The Phenomenon of Man Explained*, 51.

4. Savary, *Teilhard de Chardin's The Phenomenon of Man Explained*, 51.

5. Savary, *Teilhard de Chardin's The Phenomenon of Man Explained*, 52.

6. This description of the Surface dimension is adapted from Olson, *And God Created Wholeness*, 46–49.

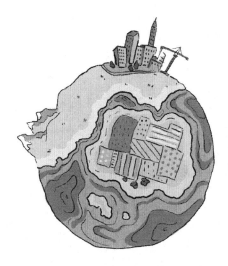

Figure 1. Surface Consciousness: The Biosphere[7]

The Surface includes the forces, laws of physics, structures, and worldviews that frame and give meaning to what is happening in the Anthropocene. In our Surface consciousness we develop a persona as a good citizen; devoted son or daughter; dedicated member of church, school, and community; reliable employee, partner, mother, or father; and ethical professional. We help our neighbors and improve the moral culture and social systems in which we live. We pursue the good, true, and beautiful with Surface consciousness.

> *Reader Reflection: What is the major focus of your Surface consciousness? Is it life-affirming? How so?*

Surface consciousness pulls together and unifies what emerges from our senses. It connects our thinking and sensing capabilities with our intuitive and emotional ability to develop metaphors and worldviews to find meaning and foster novelty. It brings the information, energy, intelligence, and matter in the universe into a coherent whole.

Our Surface consciousness tells us how other people view us. We receive feedback about our impact on others, which we can compare to our intent. We develop empathy and understanding of the perspective of

---

7. Illustration by Tuesday Hadden.

others.[8] Unfortunately, our current existential crises are a consequence of the worldview and paradigms we have constructed and play out in Surface consciousness.

LIMINAL (POSITIVE AND NEGATIVE) CONSCIOUSNESS

The word *liminal* is derived from the Latin root *limen*, which means threshold. It is a state of transition in the quantum biology model of life. The turbulent state of gases and liquids in all living cells are a threshold of innumerable, continual chemical transmissions between the Surface of life and the underlying quantum Bedrock. For psychologists,[9] the liminal space is where the persona (the Surface self) breaks down in the interest of enlarging one's larger Self (*Figure 2*).

Figure 2. Liminal Consciousness[10]

When in Liminal consciousness, we are in an emotional state where our feelings can be positive, negative, or mixed. Both Liminal-Positive and Liminal-Negative are transition zones in which we wrestle with letting go of the unwanted attachments of Surface consciousness and gain a measure of freedom from our persona.[11]

8. Eurich, *What Self-Awareness Really Is.*
9. Homans, *Jung in Context.*
10. Illustration by Tuesday Hadden.
11. Pereira, Jr., et al., "Consciousness and Cosmos."

Our emotions are not hormonal and neuronal reactions in the brain.[12] Emotions emanate from the heart and gut, and then the brain has its reaction and names them. See *Chapter 2: What the Brain Does and Does Not* for further discussion of this phenomenon.

Liminal consciousness is a space of vulnerability and uncertainty as we transition from Surface awareness to a deeper symbolic, mystical grasp of reality. Twilight or dusk, when day becomes night, is a useful metaphor to understand the depth of Liminal consciousness. Just before dark, we can see things with our eyes (called Civil twilight). Later we can see stars (Nautical twilight). Finally, we can see the faint "stars" that are really galaxies (Astronomical twilight).

Many in our spiritual traditions enhance their emotional transition into these liminal states by chanting, fasting, or doing yoga, tai chi, or chi gong; or using psychedelics, sacred plants, extreme temperatures, sleep deprivation, Tibetan brass bowls, and crystals.[13]

Whatever emerges in the liminal state is intended for our personal growth, whether we experience it as positive or negative. Ideally, Liminal consciousness enables us to act with calm and care to maximize our happiness and compassion for others. The dynamics of moving in and out of liminal awareness is demonstrated in *Chapter 7: Moving Between Dimensions of Consciousness*.

> *Reader Reflection: Think of times when you were in a liminal state, perhaps when you were just waking up. What kinds of images "popped into your head?" Did you experience these images as positive or negative or both? Did they seem to be real? The Liminal is likely giving you an invitation to explore in your Surface consciousness.*

BEDROCK CONSCIOUSNESS

Quantum biologists call the fundamental source of consciousness the "Bedrock" *(Figure 3)*. This is the realm of the quantum particles of energy that are in a continual state of possibility in the Universe. In psychological terms, the Bedrock would be our unconscious: our dreams and our shadow self, the part of us that we do not own. The shadow is the hidden, denied aspects of ourselves of which we are ashamed or afraid.

---

12. www.heartmath.com
13. Sheldrake, *Ways to Go Beyond*.

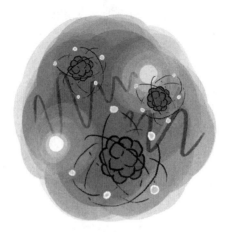

Figure 3. Bedrock Consciousness[14]

I access my Bedrock consciousness when in meditation or centering prayer, or any activity that turns off my "monkey mind," my ego, and watchful waking Surface consciousness. My "sixth sense," my intuition, is awakened.

INTUITION

Intuitions are words or images that quickly arise from our depths to our Surface consciousness to reveal the reality of what is happening and/or what is needed. Too often we dismiss or undervalue our intuition. Intuitions are practical gifts, " . . . our thinking is just noise and clutter and repetitive self-talk, while our intuitions are mostly quite relevant, as well as being delivered without fluff, streamlined down to what's essential."[15]

Einstein (1931) said:

> I believe in intuition and inspiration. . . . At times I feel certain I am right while not knowing the reason. . . . Imagination is more important than knowledge. For knowledge is limited, whereas imagination embraces the entire world, stimulating progress, giving birth to evolution.[16]

14. Illustration by Tuesday Hadden.

15. Masters, *The Anatomy of Intuition.*

16. Albert Einstein and George Bernard Shaw. *Einstein on Cosmic Religion and Other Opinions and Aphorisms.* Dover Publications Dover edition, 2009.

Einstein's insights provided purpose and direction to his empirical and theoretical work. They told him what to look for.

We have eruptions of intuition, flashes of insight, "Eureka" moments from a place where we have no control, where there is no thought. These epiphanies and ecstatic experiences can result in a profound, altered state of consciousness. When we have insights about "something more," we experience a life force that jolts us into the affirmation that whatever this is, it matters—it's serious.[17]

Our intuitive sense opens us to the limitless possibilities of Consciousness, the field of potentiality encompassing all possible manifestations, whether material or mental.[18] We can intentionally enter this state through meditation, prayer, contemplation, worship, or dreaming. Once experienced, we connect the revelation to our conscious mind to discern meaning and guidance for our actions.

> *Reader Reflection: Think of an example of something that occurred to you "out of the blue," perhaps when taking a shower. Did it turn out to be valuable? Where do you think it came from?*

INDRA'S NET: INTERRELATEDNESS OF THE DIMENSIONS OF CONSCIOUSNESS

When I developed the Wholeness Model in *And God Created Wholeness*, I speculated about what came before the quantum particles in Bedrock consciousness, if anything. Many scientists and theologians describe reality before creation of the universe as silence, darkness, mystery, nothingness, the cloud of unknowing, sacred nothingness, the unknowable, or the initial void.

The initial conditions may have been fields of creativity of quantum particles that popped in and out of being.[19] Nobel Laureate Frank Wilczek provides a mathematical explanation of the quantum fields of subatomic particles, electromagnetism, gravity, the nuclear forces, the Higgs field that gives mass to everything, and how everything interacts with light and radiation. The equations provide a firm foundation for all the physical sciences. But the equations don't account for dark energy and dark matter, which

---

17. Bell, *Love Wins.*

18. Pereira, Jr., et al., "Consciousness and Cosmos."

19. Olson and Crowell, "Self-Creating and Quantum Theories."

comprise 96 percent of the known universe, or address the possibility that there is a deeper unity that links everything together.[20]

I believe that deeper unity is Consciousness. A metaphor that depicts how Consciousness links everything together is Indra's Net (*Figure* 4).

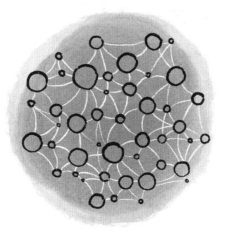

Figure 4. Indra's Net[21]

In Buddhist and Hindu cosmology, "Indra's net" is an infinitely large net of cords possessed by the deva *Indra*. In this metaphor, there is a multi-faceted jewel at each connection in the net. Each jewel is reflected in all the other jewels—a profound metaphor for the nature of reality.

> Imagine a vast net; at each crossing point there is a jewel; each jewel is perfectly clear and reflects all the other jewels in the net, the way two mirrors placed opposite each other will reflect an image ad infinitum. The jewel in this metaphor stands for an individual being, or an individual consciousness, or a cell or an atom. Every jewel is intimately connected with all other jewels in the universe, and a change in one jewel means a change, however slight, in every other jewel.[22]

This holographic metaphor describes how nature and the universe are in a continual state of relationship, emerging, unfolding, enfolding,

---

20. Wilczek, *A Beautiful Question,* 277.
21. Illustration by Tuesday Hadden.
22. From Mitchell, *The Enlightened Mind.*

and unfolding again in a never-ending cycle of renewal and transformation. Similarly, when we are in Liminal consciousness, we are in a state of emergence, a state of possibilities between Surface consciousness and deep Bedrock consciousness.

We exchange our liminal thoughts, aspirations, and creativity in Surface consciousness, and also with Bedrock consciousness where mind and thought patterns are suspended in a generative and creative space that allows for new perceptions, a shift in the content of our consciousness, including a shift in meaning and the possibilities for personal and global transformation.

Light, across all visible or nonvisible colors of the spectrum, is still essentially light, different only in the frequency of oscillation.[23] Similarly, the differences between consciousness at the Surface, Liminal, and Bedrock dimensions is one of degree of awareness.

THE "HARD PROBLEM"

Explaining any of the three dimensions of Surface, Liminal, and Bedrock consciousness is difficult for both scientists and the average person—anyone who believes that physical stuff (matter and energy) is fundamental. This materialistic worldview is seen as self-evident. After all, if the Big Bang were an explosion of physical stuff, how could Consciousness have been present?

This belief is called "physicalism," the current foundational paradigm underlying all the paradigms for much of science and everyday living. It says that the universe is fundamentally made of physical stuff called "matter."[24] In this paradigm, consciousness is part of the accidental and random evolutionary process, an emergent, inherent property of nature.[25]

This is the "hard problem" of consciousness.[26] The academic disciplines of physics and biology cannot define consciousness or mind, either as an emergent property of the brain or as an external reality that engages with the brain. It is generally denied by science because it is difficult to prove and capture within the limits of scientific concepts, methods, or even the vocabulary needed to define consciousness.

23. Metaphor of light from Kastrup, *Decoding Jung's Metaphysics*, 82.

24. Gober, *An End to Upside Down Living*, 3.

25. Gober, *An End to Upside Down Living*, 4.

26. Chalmers, "Consciousness and Its Place in Nature."

Accepting that Consciousness is fundamental will require a fundamental change in our understanding of science itself. Beginning with Galileo, science has put consciousness outside of scientific inquiry. Galileo defined the material world by size, shape, location, and motion. He described everything in mathematical language[27] and asserted that everything is governed by natural law.[28]

> Galileo's error was to commit us to a . . . theory of nature which entailed that consciousness was essentially and inevitably mysterious. In other words, Galileo created the problem of consciousness.[29]

Galileo's contribution to the scientific method advanced ways to determine truth, but it also limited our understanding of reality to a three-dimensional material world. We see and interpret the world around us as material bodies, energy, waves, and force fields (electromagnetic and gravity). Consciousness is believed to be a derivative of the brain. But the brain and all our sensory organs are derived from and supported by Consciousness,[30] as we explore in *Chapter 2: What the Brain Does and Does Not* and *Chapter 3: Universal Consciousness.*[31]

> *Reader Reflection: Reflect on your understanding of your mind. If your mind, with its perpetual questions, ideas, and lists of things to do, is not generated by your brain, what is its source?*

27. Goff, *Galileo's Error.*

28. Kauffman, *Reinventing the Sacred.*

29. Goff, *Galileo's Error,* 21–22.

30. Pereira, and Reddy, *The Manifestation of Consciousness,* 51–55.

31. For an excellent explanation of how we create our reality see Hofstadter, *I Am a Strange Loop.*

Chapter 2

WHAT THE BRAIN DOES
AND DOES NOT

FUNCTIONS OF THE BRAIN

WE THINK THAT OUR CONSCIOUSNESS is produced by our brains because the 10 billion neural networks of the brain perform 1018 operations per second. But the heart has more neurons and a much stronger magnetic field—3,000 times bigger—than the brain. Information sent from the heart to the brain is more voluminous than the information sent from the brain to the heart. The brain assigns language to the signals from the heart.[1] Our "gut," our long-winding digestive tract, also has an extremely high density of neurons that send messages to the brain.

The brain, the heart, and the gut all contribute to our overall consciousness.[2] Each electron, neuron, and cell in our body knows how to be an electron, neuron, and cell,[3] but their interactions, including the networks in the brain, *do not produce consciousness.*

Robert Epstein, the former editor-in-chief of *Psychology Today*, explains:[4]

---

1. Alexander and Newell, *Explore the Near-Death Experience,* Module Three.
2. Beichler, *Consciousness Manifesto,* 22.
3. Hofstadter, *I Am a Strange Loop.*
4. Epstein, "The Empty Brain."

> No matter how hard they try, brain scientists and cognitive psychologists will never find a copy of Beethoven's 5th Symphony in the brain—or copies of words, pictures, grammatical rules or any other kinds of environmental stimuli. The human brain isn't really empty, of course. But it does *not* contain most of the things people think it does—not even simple things such as memories.

We don't *store* words or the rules that tell us how to manipulate them. We don't create *representations* of visual stimuli, *store* them in a short-term memory buffer, and then *transfer* the representation into a long-term memory device. We don't *retrieve* information or images or words from memory registers. Computers do all these things, but organisms do not.

The neocortex of the brain, the outer surface, acts as a filter, allowing into our Surface consciousness only the information from Consciousness that is necessary and useful for our survival and improvement.[5]

The origin of the filter theory of the brain is attributed to William James, the Harvard father of psychology. James proposed that the brain acts as a partial barrier and gives us only what is possible for us to perceive. In this theory, the brain selects signals from Consciousness, filters them, and reduces them so they can fit into an individual's experience and worldview.[6]

When the brain's filter is even moderately opened, we experience feelings of unconditional joy and profound connection. The distinctions between oneself and others dissolve so the self and body are felt to be part of a greater stream of Consciousness.[7] We can also imagine the brain as an antenna with a narrow bandwidth, just as in each moment we can only see clearly what is directly in front of our eyes.

The brain's main job is running a budget for your body to keep you alive and healthy. The brain anticipates the needs of your body and meets those needs before they arrive, and budgets glucose, oxygen, salt, and all the nutrients that your body needs.[8]

Every action you take—every movement you make, every new thing you learn—costs something. And so (your brain asks itself, figuratively), is this a good investment? Is it worth it? In effect:

5. Woollacott, *Infinite Awareness*, 216.

6. James, *Human Immortality*.

7. We make contact with consciousness in the world at large. We see everything as the contents of the great mind. There is a great mind that contains the little minds of each one of us. Each little mind experiences the universe from its own vantage point, making of sensory experiences whatever it will. Marshall, *Mystical Encounters*.

8. Barrett, *Seven and a Half Lessons*.

... [T]he brain draws on your deep backlog of experience and memory, constructing what it believes to be your reality, cross-referencing it with incoming sense data from your heart, lungs, metabolism, immune system, as well as the surrounding world, and adjusting as needed. You are almost always acting on the predictions that your brain is making about what's going to happen next, not reacting to experience as it unfolds.[9]

QUANTUM REALITY

As I began to write these chapters about consciousness, these words echoed in a dream: *Discover the tunnels to the universe.*

I woke up feeling this was an important message about associating "tunneling" with what I have learned from the quantum biologists: In order to pass through barriers, quantum particles must remain in a wavy state. The electron waves pass through energy barriers like sound waves passing through walls. The quantum biologists call this "tunneling."[10]

Just as quantum particles need to be in waves to tunnel through impenetrable barriers, I interpreted the dream to mean that we need to be in a fluid and open wave state, without fixed boundaries, to tunnel through barriers to Consciousness. A quantum scientific explanation for this phenomenon would be: an electron in our brain must behave as a wave to access external Consciousness. As a wave, the electron can then travel independent of space-time similar to electrons that are entangled.[11] From this perspective, our brains have multidimensional surfaces that are connected at all points in space and time.

How does the brain (or mind) bind together millions of transactions between the neurons into an experience of a perceptual whole? How does a sense of the "I" or "self" and a perceived coherence of one's reality emerge from a biological system consisting of billions of neurons?

Large-scale, coherent electrical fields across the brain could explain how a large number of disparate and distant neurons can integrate their

9. Barrett, *Seven and a Half Lessons.*

10. This may explain how billions of protons in the cells within a tadpole work together to tunnel through strong long ropes of proteins and accelerate the production of a frog. The vibrations of the tadpole's enzymes bring atoms and molecules into close enough proximity to allow electrons and protons to quantum tunnel. McFadden and Al-Khalili, *Life on the Edge,* 67.

11. Bhadra, *The Complex Quantum-State of Consciousness,* 58–93.

information to produce a holistic picture. Non-local quantum correlations (quantum entanglement) exist between particles separated in space and time. Bhadra explains:

> The world we experience becomes enriched with feelings and sensations that lend meaning to life, situate us in the context of the cosmos. We not only know but come to feel that we are an intrinsic part of the web of life, an intrinsic part of an organically whole universe.[12]

When we intentionally "tunnel" into one of the dimensions of consciousness, we disrupt our normal brain processes, empty our mind of thought, and reduce the brain's filtering of Consciousness. We precipitate extra sensory mystical experiences. We encounter the presence of intelligence at the heart of religious and spiritual systems.

Stuart Hameroff and Deepak Chopra believe that the concept of a "quantum soul" is scientifically plausible. If so, this would suggest that our quantum consciousness is interconnected via entanglement among all living beings and the universe, that cosmic wisdom/Platonic values are embedded as quantum information, and that consciousness is able to exist at deeper planes and scales independent of biology. With the advent of quantum biology, non-locality must be taken seriously as a possible bridge between science and spirituality.[13]

Consciousness is the transpersonal field that we encounter physically through our senses and brain.[14]

HOW THE BRAIN ACCESSES CONSCIOUSNESS

Meijer and Geesink offer an explanation of how our individual mind connects to Consciousness in a mental workspace that is associated with, but not reducible to, our brain.[15]

> Our brain is . . . a central part of our nervous system that exchanges information with the entire organism and the cosmos. The brain is embedded in a mental workspace that communicates

---

12. Bhadra, *The Complex Quantum-State of Consciousness*, 58–93.
13. Hameroff and Chopra, "The Quantum Soul."
14. Kastrup, "Physics is Pointing Inexorably to Mind."
15. Adapted from Meijer and Geesink, "Consciousness in the Universe, 41–79.

with the whole nervous system. Our self-consciousness operates
from . . . the presence of a field-receptive workspace.

The brain represents the world in a mental, non-material workspace
that constructs our mental models of reality by updating from Consciousness and our material world. We are usually aware of what is happening
around us—that is called awareness. But at a deeper level when we think
about that awareness, consciousness is at work.

The millions of data points from sense organs received every moment
are channeled to various, disparate areas of the brain and processed by the
computing facility of the brain. Our consciousness receives this processed
information and creates a holistic scene. It is this integration of all the processed bits of cognitive and affective information that creates a whole, the
identity as a person, the self.[16]

James Beichler also has described how our consciousness acts like an
antenna, picking up signals and information from the rest of the universe.[17]

This cacophony of extra-dimensional input and information would
simply overwhelm our brains under ordinary conditions, so it is generally
tamped down or cut out altogether by the neural networks. If the input
from the universe rises to the level of coherent thought, we call it a "gut
feeling," vision, or an extra-sensory perception (ESP) event such as synchronicity, telepathy, and precognition.

Our "higher" consciousness or spiritual "higher self" is our intuitive
capacity to sense the general wholeness and oneness of the universe, even
though our five senses (sight, sound, smell, touch, taste) in our Surface consciousness would have us believe that we are individuals separate, distinct,
and unconnected from other things in the universe.

The brain organizes the contents of consciousness "behind the scenes"
with the aid of fast, efficient, non-conscious systems that connect with
Consciousness. All this happens without any interference from our personal awareness.

Experimental evidence suggests that single cells have simple memories
in virtually the same way as neurons.[18] Cells have the necessary complexity
to receive and analyze consciousness. Even an amoeba has its own very

16 Adapted from Meijer and Geesink, "Consciousness in the Universe, 41–79.

17. The discussion of the fourth dimension is derived from Beichler, *The Consciousness Revolution in Science*. Beichler is Professor of Neurocosmology, Vetha Center for Transdisciplinary Studies.

18. Carroll, "Cellular Memory."

rudimentary kind of psyche. As living things become more complex—as their cells increase in number and become more intricately organized—they become capable of "receiving" more consciousness.[19]

In a sense, all things are alive, as many indigenous people believe, because they are all pervaded by consciousness. But there's a difference in the way that rocks and rivers are alive compared to the way that insects or an amoeba are alive. Because rocks and rivers do not have their own psyche, they are not individually conscious. Consciousness pervades them, but they are not conscious themselves, as far as we know.[20]

Depth psychologists use the term "transpersonal psyche" to describe a psyche that is able to sense a greater intelligence than our own, which manifests itself to us in the form of numinous experiences.[21]

WHAT COMES FROM CONSCIOUSNESS?

The illusion of being separate from the universe dissipates; we can perceive reality as it is, independent of our own memories and concepts.[22] There are experiences—sensations, thoughts, intuitions—that surface in our consciousness without having passed through the five senses. They reach us directly from Consciousness as spontaneous, spiritual windows to reality.

In his near-death-experience (NDE) coma, Eben Alexander did not have a properly functioning filter and so experienced a much broader contact with Consciousness.[23] Research into brain activity during transcendental experiences, such as an NDE, indicates that the brain "goes dark." Using magnetic resonance imaging (MRI), which uses oxygen from the blood as a proxy for neuronal activity, the researchers found that no part of the brain shows an increase in activity during these experiences.[24]

The research demonstrated that the more extraordinary the transcendental aspects of the experience, the darker the brain was in terms of

19. Taylor, *Spiritual Science*, 51.

20. Taylor, *Spiritual Science*, 51.

21. Corbett, *Psyche and the Sacred*, 74.

22. Corbett, *Psyche and the Sacred*, 74.

23 Alexander and Newell, *Living in a Mindful Universe*.

24. Alexander and Newell, *Living in a Mindful Universe*. Robin Carhart-Harris, Imperial College London, using not only functional MRI but even a more specific measure of neural activity in the brain, the magnetoencephalography, also found that the brain goes dark.

functional MRI measurements. The action that creates this phenomenal experience is not due to increased activity in the brain. The brain is literally getting out of the way.[25]

The metaphor of light passing through a prism being refracted into all the colors of the rainbow is useful *(Figure 5)*. Each spectral color is still the light but appears to be different from the white light entering the prism.

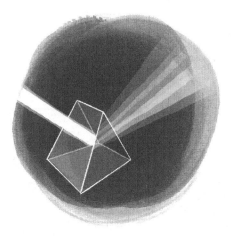

Figure 5. Prism Metaphor for Dispersion of Consciousness[26]

The light is necessary for the colors to appear. The colors are a manifestation of the light. Like the light through the prism, Universal Consciousness is dispersed to become all the manifestations we experience in all dimensions of human consciousness. When brain activity is reduced through meditation or other portals to Consciousness, the prism of the mind is transcended and light comes through, not as colors, but as the eternal truth of Universal Consciousness.

Continuing the metaphor, when we are aware of our True Self, we are awake in the light of Consciousness. We see the unity of Wholeness.

Most NDEs have a positive emotional tone and the fear of death is suspended; however, the emotional tone in some NDEs may include fear, terror, guilt, or despair. Pleasant NDEs tend to convey universal messages of compassion across religious and philosophical systems. Distressing NDEs typically have less focus but can be read as an invitation to self-examination

25 Alexander and Newell, *Explore the Near-Death Experience,* Module Three.

26. Illustration by Tuesday Hadden.

and a rearrangement of core beliefs. In practical terms, the common interpretation of the distressing NDE is that it is a message to turn one's life around. The primary effect of both positive and distressing NDEs is a powerful and enduring awareness that the physical world is not the full extent of reality.[27]

We are not separate islands of individuality but individual whirlpools in a stream of Consciousness that affects other whirlpools of consciousness when it dissipates and flows into a larger stream.

Now is the time to explore that larger stream of Universal Consciousness in greater depth in *Chapter 3*.

27. Bush and Greyson, "Distressing Near-Death Experiences."

Chapter 3

UNIVERSAL CONSCIOUSNESS

> "Beyond good and evil is a field. I will meet you there."
>
> —RUMI

THE FIELDS OF UNIVERSAL CONSCIOUSNESS

UNIVERSAL CONSCIOUSNESS IS THE NON-MATERIAL reality most easily pictured as wavy fields of quantum information that penetrate the whole of the Universe.[1] These "fields" ripple and sway and are spread everywhere. In 1846, Michael Faraday identified electric and magnetic fields. Since then, quantum field theory has identified the waves of 12 such fields that are tied up into bundles of energy called "quanta." These fields of energy and information are entangled and interacting with the energy fields in which our material bodies are embedded.[2] They are the local manifestations of something immensely more vast: Consciousness.[3]

Our world is just a local manifestation of Consciousness fields that have been reduced into forms of matter. Our bodies, which we localize in time and space, are not localized at all. We are connected to the fields of Consciousness, which are evolving as the universe evolves.

1. Meijer, et al. "Consciousness in the Universe," 72–107.

2. Oschman and Oschman, "The Heart as a Bi-directional Scalar Field Antenna," 2; Lindhard, "The Theory of Six Main Levels," 9, 1.

3. Sabbadini, *Pilgrimages to Emptiness*, 9–10.

Ilia Delio describes the fields of Consciousness as "a flow of overlapping waves that is the whole of the whole."[4] The Global Consciousness Project, started at Princeton University in 1998, indicates that the fields generated by self-consciousness interact and combine, and ultimately affect and are affected by the physical world. This is a statement of their preliminary findings:

> We do not feel that our minds are isolated within our bodies. In truth, we experience the world with beautiful intimacy, we know our loved ones from afar, and we leap in thought to the stars. Research on anomalies of consciousness shows that we may have direct communication links with each other, and intentions can have effects in the world despite physical barriers and separation.[5]

Think of Consciousness as a kind of cosmic DNA that gives meaning to all the non-material and material reality throughout the universe. Consciousness is in the quantum information and energy that pops out of nothing every billion of a trillionth of a second.[6]

Each non-human being on our planet has a consciousness in a myriad of forms vastly different from our own. Even photons have some awareness. Rocks feel the pressure before an earthquake. In the sixties, James Lovelock formulated the hypothesis that living and non-living parts of the Earth form a complex, interacting system that comprises a single organism.[7] Named after the Greek goddess Gaia, the hypothesis postulates that the biosphere regulates Earth's environment to sustain life.

Quantum physics suggests that life is joined together by the vast underwater continent of consciousness. Our conscious life is like a foam on the surface of the ocean. Underneath is an abyss of processes occurring below the threshold of our awareness.[8]

The brain interacts with Consciousness to provide a "workspace" that operates within the reality we know.[9] "Consciousness can therefore be located anywhere and everywhere but in a form that we do not understand until it takes shape within our reality."[10]

4. Delio, *The Unbearable Wholeness of Being,* 37.

5. Global Consciousness Project, *Institute of Noetic Sciences.*

6. Laszlo, *What is Reality.*

7. Lovelock, "A Physical Basis for Life Detection Experiments."

8. Laszlo, *What is Reality.*

9. Chopra and Kafatos, *You Are the Universe,* 219.

10. Pereira and Reddy, "The Manifestation of Consciousness," 51–55.

When Bishop John Shelby Spong, a major theologian of progressive Christianity, began work on his 2009 publication, *Eternal Life*, he studied the development of consciousness, then self-consciousness, and finally the possibility of Universal Consciousness. In his study of the Gospel of John, he saw Jesus as a doorway into Universal Consciousness.[11] Spong says:

> Our call is . . . to step beyond our limits into a new understanding of what it means to be human. It is to move from the status of self-consciousness to a realization that we share in a universal consciousness.[12]

The research into non-local Consciousness includes images and emotions shared between minds separated by distance, perception of distant events or images (currently or through time), and influence of distant systems via mental intention.[13]

Because subjectivity is outside the known laws of physics, it is extremely difficult for science to measure. However, even mathematicians are accepting that inanimate matter and perhaps even the universe could be conscious.[14]

DID MATERIAL REALITY COME FROM CONSCIOUSNESS?

The hard problem for the materialist is: How can consciousness emerge from physical structures? But explaining how material reality came from consciousness is also a hard problem. Were matter and mind both present as the universe evolved? Such a perspective would open a window of possibility both outside of the material frame and outside of mysticism.

The Mark Gober paradigm of Consciousness depicts that everything else in reality comes from, and is experienced, within Consciousness.[15,16] Through billions of years of evolution, Consciousness created physical matter, chemistry, biological organisms and, ultimately, brains. Figure 6 illustrates this concept.

11. Spong, *The Fourth Gospel*.

12. Spong, *The Fourth Gospel*, 206.

13. Radin, *Real Magic*.

14. Michael Brooks, "Is the Universe Conscious?"

15. Gober, *An End to Upside Down Thinking*; Di Biase, *The Unified Field of Consciousness*; Hu and Wu, *The Original Principle*.

16. Gober, *An End to Upside Down Thinking*, xxi.

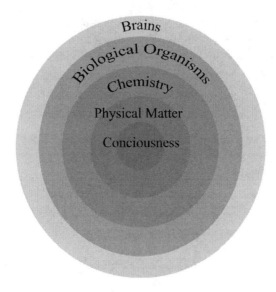

Figure 6. The New Paradigm[17]

Experimental research on consciousness in new sub-disciplines in medicine, biology, and physics have affirmed the 1931 statement by Max Planck, the father of quantum mechanics:

> I regard consciousness as fundamental. I regard matter as derivative from consciousness. We cannot get behind consciousness. Everything that we talk about, everything that we regard as existing, postulates consciousness.[18]

Many scientific papers support this paradigm of Consciousness. Dirk K.F. Meijer, a professor of pharmacokinetics at the University of Groningen, has posted the following mission statement for this paradigm:

> Further elaboration of the concept of Consciousness and its practical implications may be instrumental in changing the current mindset of humans into devoted participants in a cosmic plan. The concept may lead to the realization that everyone is part of a wholeness of astonishing size and beauty, implying the deep responsibility of each of us for the future of mankind and all that lives. It can also support current constructive activities in our societies, aimed at a brighter future for our planet.[19]

17. Illustration by Tuesday Hadden.
18. Planck, Interview in *The Observer.*
19. See Meijer, "Universal Consciousness," an open article that invites comments.

Consciousnesses is "non-local," existing independently of space and time, and is not based in the physiology of living creatures.[20] Each being is in interrelation with Consciousness, partaking of the information of the whole.[21]

CONSCIOUSNESS IN THEORIES OF CREATION

Neil Theise and Menas Kafatos propose "Fundamental Awareness" as a grand theory that integrates:

1. Western philosophical traditions,

2. Insights from culturally diverse contemplative and mystical traditions, and

3. Current scientific thinking, expressible mathematically.[22]

In this framework, Consciousness is the foundational element of all existence, not reducible to anything else.[23]

> The universe is non-material, self-organizing throughout, a holarchy of complementary, process-driven, recursive interactions.[24]

Most theories that purport to include the nature of being, reality, becoming, and existence do not describe the origin of Consciousness or its mechanics.

John Crowell[25] developed a theory of conscious self-creating change that explains the origin and mechanics of consciousness. In Crowell's theory, Consciousness guides, unifies, and transforms information and energy

---

20. Schwartz, "The Transformation."

21. Hardy, "Nonlocal Consciousness."

22. Hardy, "Nonlocal Consciousness."

23. Theise and Kafatos, *Fundamental Awareness.*

24. Theise and Kafatos, *Fundamental Awareness.*

25. John D. Crowell was New Business and New Product Development Director for the 3M Company, CEO of 3M Chile, and Technical Director of the Chemicals Division. He has a PhD in Synthetic Organic Chemistry (Florida State University). Currently an independent scholar investigating consciousness, creativity, cognition, and their relationships with the Cosmos.

into intelligence and matter.[26] Consciousness provides stability in the transition between the beginnings and endings in every physical entity—from atoms to universes, from cells to ecosystems, from neurons to the totality of the networks of intelligence in all ordered existence.[27] Lex Neale's theory of "Integral Relativity" supports the Crowell theory that Consciousness is the continuing connection of Energy, Mind, and Matter.[28]

Dean Radin, who is the chief scientist at the Institute of Noetic Sciences, traces the concept of Universal Consciousness back to the god Hermes/ Mercury, who was considered an emissary between the gods and humans.[29] The notion of an "emissary" between the human and the divine resonates with Consciousness as a connector in the theories of Crowell and Neale.

EVOLUTION OF CONSCIOUSNESS

Try this thought exercise: Imagine placing a dot of ink on a folded piece of tissue paper. Think of the dot as the moment of creation. The ink permeates all of the folds of the tissue. Now imagine unfolding the tissue. What do you see? As the Universe spread out, the matter appeared throughout the universe, as do the dots in the tissue. The tissue that connects all the dots is Consciousness.[30]

Scientists call the space between the galaxies and stars "dark energy." Is it a form of Consciousness that we can't see?

> Whether one is a terrorist or a piano tuner, a murderer or a mystic, the very same force is within each individual, holding the atoms and cells together, unifying us in the web of existence. . . . When Einstein reached the conclusions that 'something deeply hidden had to be behind things,' it is this force he was talking about.[31]

---

26. Compare this statement with Richard Rohr's comment: "You could say that God's only and forever pattern is *creatio ex nihilo*: Yahweh is always "creating something out of nothing." Christian words for the same eternal pattern are "resurrection' and 'grace." In *Things Hidden: Scripture as Spirituality,* 90.

27. For a more complete description of the Crowell theory contact Dr. Crowell at johncrowell@aol.com

28. Neale, "Integral Relativity of Awareness and Energy," 173.

29. Radin, *Real Magic,* 49.

30. Thanks to Dr. Eric A. Olson for suggesting the ink dot exercise.

31. Phillips, *No Ordinary Time,* 196.

Our minds have evolved within a strictly three-dimensional, external, material, physical world, but Consciousness is a greater multi-dimensional world that is constantly changing and becoming more complex over time. The transpersonal and quantum state of Consciousness is beyond the space and time of our three-dimensional world.

Life on the planet emerged from the complexity of quantum interactions. Shantena Sabbadini, a theoretical physicist who contributed to the first identification of a black hole, describes the interactions of "quantum indeterminacy" (uncertainty) and the determinism (certainty) of the physical laws of the universe:

> Life is the rich interplay of quantum indeterminacy with the determinism of physical laws that create this fantastic universe, including the amazing phenomenon that we are. The freedom of the living is quantum indeterminacy spelled big; quantum indeterminacy is life spelled small.[32]

As life became more complex, it was able to develop the mental capacities (human consciousness) to access Consciousness. In a sense, life is the Universe viewing itself.

WE ARE EXPRESSIONS OF CONSCIOUSNESS

Bernado Kastrup imagines that all of reality is a stream of water, where water represents Consciousness. The whirlpools within the stream represent individuals. Sometimes water from one whirlpool can end up in another whirlpool (think: psychic abilities). When a whirlpool dissipates, the water flows into the broader stream (think: consciousness continues when the physical body dies).[33]

Recently Kastrup and associates argued that the physical universe *as a whole* is the extrinsic appearance of a universal inner life, just as a living brain and body are the extrinsic appearance of a person's inner life. In their study of dissociative identity disorders (DID), they found that consciousness can give rise to many operationally distinct centers of concurrent experience, each with its own personality and sense of identity. They say:

> Therefore, if something analogous to DID happens at a universal level, the one universal consciousness could, as a result, give

32. Sabbadini, *Pilgrimages to Emptiness*, 129.
33. Kastrup, *Why Materialism Is Baloney*.

rise to many alters with private inner lives like yours and ours. *As such, we may all be alters—dissociated personalities—of universal consciousness . . .* We posit that this appearance is *life itself*: metabolizing organisms are simply what universal-level dissociative processes look like. [34]

If Kastrup and his associates are correct—that Consciousness can become many individual minds—there may be "an unprecedentedly coherent and empirically grounded way of making sense of life, the universe and everything."[35]

Reader Reflection: Does knowing more about the non-material reality of Consciousness totally boggle your mind, or does it help you to make sense of your beliefs and assumptions about reality?

While there is much to be learned about an empirical basis for Consciousness, we already know a lot about gaining access to Consciousness, which we explore in *Part II: Accessing Universal Consciousness.*

---

34. Kastrup, Crabtree, and Kelly, "Could Multiple Personality Disorder Explain Life, the Universe and Everything?"

35. Kastrup, Crabtree, and Kelly, "Could Multiple Personality Disorder Explain Life, the Universe and Everything?"

Part I Implications

ETHOS OF CONSCIOUSNESS

THE PRISM OF CONSCIOUSNESS

FOR CENTURIES, ELABORATE MISUNDERSTANDINGS OF reality have been promulgated by philosophers, theologians, and scientists. Most assumed that all phenomena in the world originated in the interaction of particles of matter. When the particles in enough brain cells interacted in the right way, they believed that consciousness somehow emerged. All along, Consciousness was there, interacting with a self-creating process. Consciousness connects and channels the information-intelligence and energy-matter dynamics in the universe to empower the emergence of life. .

Consciousness was there before brains began to detect it. As our bodies developed, they included brains, hearts, five senses, and a sixth sense we call intuition that interacted with the fields of self-creation and Consciousness—and created a space for our "mind."

HUMAN CONSCIOUSNESS

We have created a collective cultural human consciousness, a social reality that controls evolution on the planet: the Anthropocene. We have made up a world that exists only in human consciousness. Barrett explains:

> The Earth itself, with its rocks and trees and deserts and oceans, is physical reality. Social reality means that we impose new functions on physical things, collectively. We agree, for example, that

a particular chunk of Earth is the United States and it is carved up into 50 made-up areas called states. And sometimes we disagree. In the Middle East, for example, people kill each other over whether a parcel of land is Israel or Palestine. Even if we don't explicitly discuss social reality, our actions make it real.[1]

This collective consciousness is a superpower that can do much to evolve the planet toward wholeness. With effective leadership, the biosphere and all of the creatures therein can flourish. Or it can be destructive. It can be deluded by leaders who see personal and material gain as our Omega—our ultimate goal and destiny. Think of the idolatry of the golden calf in Exodus 32.

Or the collective human consciousness can be directed and opened to the wisdom and grace of the perennial wisdom of Consciousness, the domain of unbroken wholeness with no boundaries where the center is everywhere all the time.

Jungian analyst Steven Herrmann relates his experience after tending some redwood tree seedlings in a park during a California drought in 2013. He had this dream:[2]

> ... [T]here was an enormous redwood tree towering up right outside my window. It was enormous, and the tree spoke to me; it thanked me for doing this work.

When he awoke, he wondered if the towering tree was the soul of the redwood tree speaking to him, expressing compassion for the seedlings he had planted. He began to think that the trees might have a consciousness of their own.

He then had a series of synchronistic experiences with a house, a door, and wall paneling, all related to redwood trees that seemed to be transmitting some kind of consciousness. He said, "It changed my perception about meaning and my small place in the cosmos."[3]

This is an example of how Universal Consciousness is an organizing principle of order in the universe. Herrmann concluded that just as there is a complexity of consciousness in nature, there is "a consciousness of the spiritual self hidden away in the unconscious and matter."[4]

1. Barrett, *Seven and a Half Lessons*.
2. Herrmann, *William James and C. G. Jung*, 399.
3. Herrmann, *William James and C. G. Jung*, 401.
4. Herrmann, *William James and C. G. Jung*, 404.

THE FIRE WITHIN

At an early age, Teilhard de Chardin saw the world "becoming luminous, lit from within, like the burning bush that Moses encountered in the desert, the Divine radiating from the depths of a blazing Matter."[5] The fire Teilhard imagined was the consciousness in all matter, the energy thrumming through the universe. Consciousness is the sacred "fire" of the spirit that Teilhard imagined.

Consciousness is not simply within the material world per se, but within our human consciousness, within the 100 trillion cells of our bodies, all of which communicate with each other via chemical and electrical systems.[6] We are at a crossroads. We either open ourselves to the "fire" and embrace the inclusivity, goodness, and possibilities within, or we give in to the relentless rise of the ego to the demise of our species. Choosing this Consciousness of Wholeness is our only future.

The continued use of the Large Hadron Collider[7] to search for a grand force that underlies everything is misplaced. Consciousness is this underlying and unifying force that the scientists are looking for. Everything—atoms, galaxies, and forces like gravity—is just the manifestation of a self-creating process of change, beyond space and time, and filled with creative potential.

We have the freedom to choose. If we locate Consciousness within, we take it on as our ethos. We relate to each other and the world with Consciousness.

5. Teilhard De Chardin, *The Heart of Matter*, 16.

6. Fredriksson, ed., *The Mysteries of Consciousness*.

7. The Large Hadron Collider (LHC) is the world's largest and highest-energy particle collider, located in a tunnel beneath the France-Switzerland border near Geneva. It was built to allow physicists to test predictions of theories of particle physics and to search for the new particles predicted by supersymmetric theories.

Part II

ACCESSING UNIVERSAL CONSCIOUSNESS

INTRODUCTION: MYSTICAL EXPERIENCES

> "As I have gained knowledge and seen others share their visions
> with me, I conclude that our ancestors lived in a strange condition
> in which they were in touch with the spirits constantly, and I see that
> as a goal for our present activities."[1]
>
> —VINE DELORIA

VINE DELORIA, A RENOWNED NATIVE American scholar, suggests that
transforming the Anthropocene will require us to be "in touch with the
spirits constantly." Translated to our focus on Consciousness, this means we
must embrace the reality of mystical, transcendental, and spiritual intuition
as a source of valuable knowledge.

These chapters are about accessing Consciousness, the eternal energy
that makes us immortal, living spirits and vitalizes society. Accessing Consciousness offers a deeper dimension of perception—a mythical dimension. Consciousness is always present, here and now. Our opportunity is to
access and promote Consciousness.

Prayer, especially Centering Prayer, and meditation are the most
commonly used means of accessing Consciousness. For many, prayer and
meditation are sufficient to bring them to a mystical, transcendent, and

1. Deloria, *God is Red.*

transformative space where they are "in touch" with the Divine, Spirit, God, Jesus, Allah, or other manifestations of Consciousness.

To reach the goal of being in constant touch with Consciousness, additional and more radical approaches are needed. In these chapters, readers are asked to explore, reflect, and critically analyze their own mystical and spiritual experience with additional portals to Consciousness. The doorways to Universal Consciousness may be found within everyone. Some involve religious figures, but all doorways are passageways "to a deeper and infinitely unknowable experience of the Self."[2]

Chapter 4: Experiencing the Mystical. We explore the capacity to be mystical, to say "yes" to a sense of awe, wonder, and beauty that is essential for moving beyond our material, ego-driven worldviews.

Chapter 5: Dream Portals to Consciousness. Dreams are the portals to Consciousness that have had the greatest impact on history and offer a great hope for a viable future.

Chapter 6: Waking Portals to Consciousness. Along with prayer and meditation, the portals of sounds, music, symbols, and stories are some of the ways we can open to the higher frequencies in the universe.

Chapter 7: Moving Between the Dimensions of Consciousness. To develop both personal and collective wholeness, accessing all dimensions of Consciousness and intently moving between them is essential for developing our human consciousness and participating in the continued development of Universal Consciousness.

Teilhard's search for wholeness in the dynamics of evolution points to a new understanding of God and a new understanding of ourselves in relation to God. The following poetic expression of the Source by Ilia Delio is a way of understanding God and Consciousness.

> The name *God* points to the mystery of an unspeakable source of eternal love that flows endlessly from the divine creative heart into the mouth of creation, an eternal divine kiss that is, at once, a deep intimate presence.[3]

> [Jesus'] . . . deep interior oneness with God expressed itself in a consciousness of the whole. . . . God thrives in between the

---

2. Herrmann, *William James and C.G. Jung,* 384.

3. Delio, *Hours of the Universe,* xvii.

known and the unknown, between uncertainty and hope, stretching forth into the world as our souls expand with new levels of consciousness.[4]

Consciousness gives us the wisdom that works with our intuition to experience more than what is possible with our five senses. This connection to Consciousness can be anything from self-knowledge to cosmic knowledge. The feeling is a strong, sometimes overpowering, feeling that the information is valid, authentic, and true, despite its purely subjective nature.[5]

To expand your openness to absorb the following mystical chapters, read the following story by Peter Tompkins and Christopher Bird in *The Secret Life of Plants*:

> To see if a plant could display memory, six blindfolded polygraph students drew folded strips of paper from a hat. One of them contained instructions to root up, stamp on, and thoroughly destroy one of the two plants in a room. The criminal was to commit the crime in secret. No one knew his identity, and only the second plant would be a witness. When the surviving plant was attached to a polygraph, the students paraded before it one by one. The plant gave no reaction to five of them, but when the actual culprit approached, the meter went wild.[6]

4. Delio, *Hours of the Universe*, 9–11.

5. Hood, "The Construction and Preliminary Validation," 29.

6. Tompkins and Bird, *The Secret Life of Plants*.

Chapter 4

EXPERIENCING THE MYSTICAL

"The most beautiful and most profound experience is the sensation of the mystical. It is the sower of all true science. He to whom this emotion is a stranger, who can no longer wonder and stand rapt in awe, is as good as dead. To know that what is impenetrable to us really exists, manifesting itself as the highest wisdom and the most radiant beauty which our dull faculties can comprehend only in their primitive forms—this knowledge, this feeling is at the center of true religiousness."[1]

—ALBERT EINSTEIN

EINSTEIN SAID THAT THE "MYSTICAL sensation" is the most beautiful and most profound experience. If we haven't had these experiences, "we are as good as dead." Rather strong and poetic language by an eminent scientist to access "the highest wisdom and the most radiant beauty."

We saw in *Part I* that Consciousness is hosted by the brain, like a computer is the host for a hard-drive full of information. The sub-atomic particles like quarks in our cells communicate through flashes of light. It is not surprising that the disciples of Christ on Pentecost called the light on top of their heads "tongues of fire"—the only way light could be described in those days (think of Moses and the burning bush). There were

---

1. Einstein, "The Merging of the Spirit and Science," 108.

36

no flashlights, only candles (tongues of fire).[2] The disciples had a mystical experience.

THIN PLACES

The boundary between Liminal consciousness and Bedrock consciousness is incredibly soft, porous, and permeable as the brain's filter opens, and we are in touch with Universal Consciousness. We are then in a "thin place,"[3] where the material world is seen as the phenomenal representation of a much deeper universal reality. The imaginal realm points toward a higher vision of our human purpose that is both evolutionary and collective.[4]

We may encounter a thin place in nature, music, poetry, dance, or worship. It could be a new relationship, seeing the sky at night, or witnessing the birth of a child. When we become vulnerable and broken from sickness, loss of a loved one, or poor choices, we move into a thin place.

Thin places produce an intense feeling that there is something that cannot be seen—a tipping point, epiphany, or personal revelation that triggers emotions and transformation. We may get 'goose bumps' when we experience awe or feel we are in a sacred place. They are magical moments in which we are struck by the wonderment of life. This is all mystical territory.

The "Eureka" discoveries of scientists or creative insights we have in dreams or while taking a shower are Liminal mystical times. We experience the all-encompassing unity, knowledge, vision, and love of the eternal and cosmic Self. The illusion of being separate is lifted. The insights we gain in these liminal mystical thin places motivates us to use these insights as a force for good. It is this integration of mystical insights and exercising power in Surface consciousness that fuels the work of prophets and mystics.[5]

The link between mystical liminal reality and life in the material world is made clearer in my dream:

> I am swimming in a lake when I notice a family setting up a picnic
> at the bottom of the lake. It was the same configuration they had

2. "When the day of Pentecost came, they were all together in one place. Suddenly a sound like the blowing of a violent wind came from heaven and filled the whole house where they were sitting. They saw what seemed to be tongues of fire that separated and came to rest on each of them." Acts 2:1–3.

3. Borg, *The Heart of Christianity*.

4. Bourgeault, *Eye of the Heart*.

5. Phillips, *No Ordinary Time*, 197.

on the shore, but they moved it to the lake bottom. I swam, going from the shallow to the deep water and back to the shore. I was thinking about the seasons when swimming was possible.[6]

The dream suggests that what we do in our waking life exists as possibilities in the mystical reality of Bedrock consciousness. We create our reality as we connect to Consciousness. The ideas that form are acted out in the material world.

In his near-death experience (NDE), Eben Alexander witnessed schools of flying fish down in the water, living in a material realm. He said, "This is where we're here to learn and teach these profound lessons of growth." The beautiful schools of flying fish that would then pop up out of the water, gliding in the air above the wavetops are "an analogy to our being between lives." The imagery of the flying fish going in and out of the water was a vast complex of interactive nodes that showed Alexander how all the important work of the universe, which is the evolution of consciousness itself, was derived from those relationships that we share. He said, "The relationships were like a multi-layered tapestry."[7]

Although I interpreted the water in my dream as Bedrock consciousness and life on land as Surface consciousness, the dynamics in my dream and Alexander's NDE is the movement between interactive realms that describes the evolution of consciousness as the interplay of the material and spiritual worlds.

At a certain point we need to transition from being "seekers" of transformation to being active practitioners. Thinking and talking about change, debating fine points and strategies is fine, but there comes a point when we must act. How can we best proceed? What actions are practical, genuine, and sustainable?

MYSTICAL EXPERIENCES

Developing and maintaining a deep connection to Consciousness is most likely to have a positive impact on others. Jesus' power to get fishermen to leave their nets and follow him is an example of this deep connection. Eben Alexander had this experience when he met Ram Dass. As Alexander came closer to Dass, he felt his heart swelling with pure love energy that seemed

---

6. Olson, *And God Created Wholeness.*

7. Alexander and Newell, *Explore the Near-Death Experience,* Module Five.

to be coming from Ram Dass himself as he looked at Alexander "with clear pure intent."[8]

This was my experience when I met with the Imam Feisal Abdul Rauf at Chautauqua Institution. I immediately had the sense that I could have followed him as a disciple if I had met him in an earlier time. I sensed that he was connected to Universal Consciousness, which he calls Allah.

For many, their first and most powerful experience with mysticism is in an encounter with well-known mystics. These are two comments from participants in my recent course on Consciousness:

> I heard the Dali Lama in a Zoom meeting. I could feel my heart enlarge.

> Sadguru is deeply mystical but very present in the world. I am aware of being in the presence of a special person. When he is with you, he is totally present but there is no attachment. You are totally embraced—a powerful experience.

> *Reader Reflection: Have you ever met someone so deeply spiritual that you sensed they were in regular contact with another reality? How was that experience for you?*

We all have the capacity to be compelling for others. The "guru" is within us.

Mystical experiences are phenomena that emerge when our waking consciousness is not processing input from the three-dimensional world, such as during sleep or deep meditation. The brain then takes in information from another dimension of space/time: Universal Consciousness.

Not everyone trusts their mystical experience because it does not fit their worldview or because they have seen the negative consequences when religious literalists have used mystical experiences to reinforce their literalism. Some have reported the experience of receiving a massage for the first time. Pent-up emotions are released, energy is felt flowing up and down the body, or buried memories or visions pop-up.

These experiences may be intense, but on a scale of intensity (*Table 1*), they are at the low end.

---

8. Alexander and Newell, *Living in a Mindful Universe*, 230.

Table 1. Continuum of the Intensity of Mystical Experience

Minimal Intensity			Maximum Intensity
Intuition "Gut feeling"	Meaningful Coincidences	Near-Death Experiences	Full Awareness of Consciousness

Our intuition provides *low-intensity* experiences such as a sense that we know something without knowing how we know. Extra-sensory and near-death experiences are more intense and can radically change one's personality and attitudes.[9] For example, we lose our fear of death after NDEs because our brains have been rewired for more immediate contact with the reality that consciousness survives death.

Reaching enlightenment and full awareness of the reality of Consciousness are at the *high intensity* end of the scale.

We can also have a mystical experience from consciousness in our normal, everyday life. Universal Consciousness can be made known to us in the most unexpected ways and times.

For example, when I was a senior in Jackson High School (Minnesota), my parents and I lived in a two-bedroom farmhouse. My bedroom was upstairs. One evening as I walked up the stairs, I felt a strange presence weighing on me. By the time I got to my bed I was overwhelmed by that presence and driven to my knees. I saw a vision of Jesus[10] hovering over the end of the bed. All I could do was cry and wonder what was happening. Before going to sleep, I had another vision of a person (me?) being constrained because of a connection to Jesus.

The vision changed my life. I was an evangelical Christian during my freshman year in college. I remember reprimanding my English professor and "saving" my roommate. During the following summer, I gave sermons while working as a porter on the S.S. North American that cruised from Chicago to Buffalo and returned every week. After three more years of college, including becoming a philosophy major, my zeal was tempered but I

9. Some people can inherit or learn to use their natural mystical abilities as a psychic or medium. They rewire neural networks in the brain through continued practice and learning to accommodate that ability.

10. "Jesus" looked like the pictures of Jesus that were prevalent in 1950s America – an example of how Consciousness is mediated by culture.

have never forgotten the power of my "conversion." The direct, unmediated experience of a power greater than myself that was too mysterious to put into words was the beginning of my life as a mystic.

It was also the beginning of my appreciation of *gnosis*, the pure knowing that comes from experience and identification with that experience. I began to appreciate the poetic language of symbols, metaphors, parables, rituals, and sounds.

Our human consciousness is supported by Universal Consciousness just as the visible tip of an iceberg is supported by the greater base and the surrounding sea from which the iceberg was formed. Our growing mystical awareness (enLIGHTenment) can be understood as a process whereby the "light" of the conscious tip of the iceberg gradually extends into unconscious layers until there is a complete understanding that encompasses both the iceberg and the grounding sea.[11]

The "light" that will transform the iceberg lies in each individual's direct, subjective, mystical experiences. These experiences enable us to see more than one reality at the same time, which gives a depth to both our experience and to our response to the experience. With a broader worldview, feelings of separation from the world give way to a deeper interconnection with all of life. We expand our understanding of self, others, and their place in the broader universe. With profound mystical experiences, "life as usual" is no longer a viable option.[12]

Will a critical mass of leaders from every walk of life find the vision, hear the call, develop sustainable practices, find support, and embrace the trust that is needed to take appropriate actions?[13] My hope is that they will realize that their identity in Surface consciousness is NOT their True Self.

The portals to Consciousness we discuss in *Chapter 5: Dream Portals to Consciousness* and *Chapter 6: Waking Portals to Consciousness* can wake everyone up to see that their True Self is a part of Universal Consciousness.

11. Metaphor of the iceberg and consciousness adapted from Velmans, "Reflective Monism."

12. Schiltz, "Emerging Worldviews."

13. Schiltz, "Emerging Worldviews."

Chapter 5

DREAM PORTALS TO CONSCIOUSNESS

Reader Reflection: As you try to remember the important dreams you have had, what stands out now? Why is that so?

IN MY EXPERIENCE, DREAMS ARE the most useful portal to Consciousness. Dreams are the doorway to Bedrock consciousness, our inner ground where there is no ego. We detach from ego in order to identify with the Self, our connection to Consciousness. Dreams have unleashed my creativity, provided guidance in my relationships, clarified my life purpose, and improved my emotional and physical health. The more I pay attention to my dreams, the more I am connected to Consciousness and my True Self. Carl Jung said:

> The dream is a little hidden door in the innermost and most secret recesses of the soul, opening into that cosmic night which was psyche long before there was any ego-consciousness, and which will remain psyche no matter how far our ego-consciousness extends.[1]

My interest in dreams began while in therapy in the seventies. I read books and articles, attended workshops, and watched videos. Many important ideas and scientific breakthroughs have come directly out of dreams. The Bible is replete with accounts of important dreams. The religious beliefs and practices in virtually every cultural community recognize the value of dreams and dreaming.

1. Jung, "The Meaning of Psychology for Modern Man."

Dreaming is essential for healthy human functioning and development, for discovering the deepest realms of their psyches and developing bonds with families, communities, natural environments, religious traditions, and ultimately the cosmos itself. Dreams are experiential portals to psychological growth and spiritual enlightenment.[2]

When I dream, my sense of self in Surface consciousness is suspended and replaced by True Self in Bedrock consciousness that has no persona, space, or temporal boundaries. Since my dreams are often contradictory, paradoxical, or illogical, they are usually creative. Premonition dreams and dreams I share with my wife are evidence that each person's dreams are infinite, transcendent, unbounded, and aligned with the consciousness of others.[3]

For both Sigmund Freud and Jung, the dream was viewed as a riddle emanating from the individual's unconscious, holding a hidden meaning that needs to be deciphered. They interpreted their clients' dreams using their own theory of dreams. While much has changed in psychoanalysis since the 1900s, interpretation is still the predominant tool in dream analysis.

THE SOURCE OF DREAMS

Many people believe dreams are created as the brain randomly throws together memories and recent experiences. Freud and the many psychoanalysts after him believe that dreams were accessed through embodied imagination. The paradigm of Consciousness would suggest that dreams are created in our brain's workspace by the dreamer while linked to Consciousness.

I recently had this short dream: *Find truth in source.*

The source of dreams is Consciousness. The dream figures, and the feelings and sensations they evoke, bring the dreamer into relationship with Consciousness. Dreams are "something unbidden that come out of darkness with an intelligence beyond our waking intelligence to grasp."[4]

---

2. Bulkeley, *Dreaming in the World's Religions*, 269.

3. Dossey, *One Mind*, 231.

4. Blake, *A Gymnasium of Beliefs.*

They reveal that what is playing out in the outside world is a reflection of an archetypal process happening deep within the human psyche.[5]

Our ancestors were dependent on night dreams, daydreams, and shamanic journeys. The shaman would go into a "land of dreams" to find out what the dreams meant and how to transform the dreams for the benefit of everyone.

Dreaming gives us access to sources of knowledge and wisdom beyond the ordinary mind. They show us the future, preparing us for challenges and opportunities that lie ahead. They show us the state of our emotional and spiritual health, and then diagnose symptoms that may be developing and provide a source of imagery for self-healing.[6]

DREAMS REVEAL OUR TRUE SELF AND PURPOSE

Dreams help us to transcend ourselves and experience ourselves as part of a larger Whole. Dreams are a way in which our True Self holds up a mirror to us and says, "This is my take on what's really going on." Dreams tell us what we truly desire; they don't simply feed the ego of our Surface consciousness. They also show us how to survive what's going on around us and possible ways of navigating the future.[7]

In the final analysis, writes Carl Jung, our lives count for something only as we are related to that which is greater than we, by whatever image or name we choose to evoke and honor; if we are not related to such, our life is wasted. Evoking the image of living spirit, he concludes:

> The living spirit grows and . . . is eternally renewed and pursues its goal in manifold and inconceivable ways throughout the history of mankind. Measured against it, the names and forms which men have given it mean very little; they are only the changing leaves and blossoms on the stem of the eternal tree.[8]

For example, I recently had this dream that fostered my personal growth:

> I am driving some teenagers. They leave and a female police officer wants to inspect the car. I tell her to go ahead. I have nothing to

5. Levy, *The Quantum Revelation.*
6. Moss, *Growing Big Dreams,* 18.
7. Moss, *Growing Big Dreams,* 18.
8. Jung, *Modern Man.*

44

hide, but before one of the teenagers left, I'd said, don't look in there. That made the officer suspicious.

My immediate reflection on the dream was that people (some with impressive credentials) are inspecting this book. I am open to being analyzed in the dream, even though I may be insecure about my knowledge of some topics in this book. Upon further reflection, I believe the officer is an anima figure urging me to be completely open about my blind spots. As Socrates said, "The unexamined life is not worth living."

PORTALS TO CONSCIOUSNESS

There are four types of dreams that take us deep into Consciousness: Lucid, Prophetic, Directive, and World dreams.

Lucid Dreams

Lucid liminal dreaming is a post-dream state in between dreaming and waking. During a typical dream, the dreamer relates to the content of the dream as if it existed objectively, separate from the dreamer's self. The dreamer then reacts to figures and images within the dream as if they are other than his/her own.[9]

Lucid dreams move the dreamer to a borderline state of diminished Surface (ego) consciousness, providing opportunities to open to the in-between world of the *mundus imaginalis*, the subtle imaginal realm "which exists in a field between matter and mind."[10]

Dreams, like Surface consciousness, are an uninterrupted flow of sights, sounds, tastes, smells, tactile sensations, and thoughts. When we become lucid (wakened) in a dream, we are able to co-create with Consciousness. We are able to creatively flow with the content of the dream rather than being passively entranced by its content. We have the possibility of working out unresolved issues.

For example, I had this lucid dream in late 2020:

> I am at a convention. There are several choices of sessions. I mistakenly sit in on an LGBTQ session. A lesbian friend is there. I then go to a large auditorium where a flying, mechanical robot

9. Harrell, *Imaginal Figures in Everyday Life*.
10. Harrell, *Imaginal Figures in Everyday Life*, 6.

lands on people who then throw it to others. It lands on me several times. There are entrepreneurs in the group. I realize that there is a political science convention in another part of town at a hotel I used to go to. I decide it is too far so I stay. I look at a program to see what I want to attend.

During the dream I am engaged in the action and movement. I am trying to figure out what I should be doing, what aspects of my personal and professional identity I should embrace, and what I should leave behind as I continue this mystical journey to Consciousness.

Prophetic Dreams

Prophetic dreams give the dreamer clues as to what will come to pass. We experience this as *deja vu* from already having seen the result of that experience. I still remember a dream in the seventies while preparing to drive our SUV from Maryland to Florida for a vacation with our children. Judith, my wife, couldn't go because of a work commitment. In the dream, I veered off the road into a ditch. In the seventies, Route 95 was narrow in places. I remembered the dream and was extra vigilant to stay in the lane. We got to Florida without incident, thanks to the dream.

Like most approaches to prophecy, the message isn't always clear or exact. And almost always, it is open to interpretation.

In *And God Created Wholeness*, I reported this January 2017 dream that turned out to signal an upcoming event: *Yert is the inner person.*

When I awoke, I had no immediate idea of the meaning of "yert." I then remembered the round "hippie" homes popular in the fifties referred to as "yurts." On the Internet I found that "yert" is a word or greeting used in Sparta, Tennessee, to indicate one's happiness or approval. I had never been to Sparta, but in my imagination, it could be a place like Bedrock consciousness where my innermost mind can be happy and basking in approval and perhaps free like the hippie lifestyle. In Turkey, "yert" means clan or community or extended family, so it could suggest an inner state of coherence.

In August 2017, while at the Chautauqua Institution in New York, my wife and I learned of a retirement village in Pleasant Hill, Tennessee. We visited and purchased a home there. I then found out that our post office address is Sparta, Tennessee. After we moved to Tennessee, I was visiting a friend in a hospital when I saw a woman from Sparta with a Yert t-shirt

(*Figure 7*). I asked her what it meant. She said it was a good way to start a conversation.

Figure 7. Yert T-Shirt from Sparta, Tennessee[11]

Healing Dreams

Healing dreams often have a huge impact on the dreamer. The messages from the dream are so important that they are not soon forgotten, especially if they call for some action. Some healing dreams prescribe a solution for a problem; some are even curative. These dreams are usually direct messages from Consciousness that come in the service of healing and wholeness, even the scary ones.

In the chapter on "Moral Agency" in *And God Created Wholeness*, I reported this February 6, 2017, dream:

> I am a consultant to a business executive. A woman is with me. She briefly talks about the importance of feedback. I then ask the executive, 'Would you like some feedback?' He agrees. I tell him that I know why he is such a successful negotiator. I tell him that

11. Photo by Edwin Olson.

when I asked him a question, he replied with substance and content, and he did so forcefully. I say that I was not able to respond
because he just overwhelmed me about the topic. I had nothing
else to say. After hearing this observation, his demeanor softened.
He showed me around his place. I was missing a musical instrument. We looked in case it was there.

My reflection on the dream: My feedback was not an attack on the
executive, but rather an "I" statement about his impact on me. I told him
that his manner of arguing had shut me down. In the dream this apparently
disarmed him, and he softened his approach and accepted me, even including and supporting me on my quest for something I had lost.

The dream's message is that to be a moral presence in the face of power
or opposition, the correct stance is non-violent resistance. Like the approach of Gandhi and Martin Luther King Jr., the challenge is to show the
dominant powers the impact they are having on others. By helping them
to realize that their behaviors are devastating to others, their connection to
Consciousness is stirred.

The dream was a healing dream, it showed that it is important to have
people in power positions who have a capacity for empathy and decency.
David Brooks has recently concluded that our basic floor of decency is
more fragile than we thought; any year, some new leader may come along
and bring us back to a world of no bottom.[12]

World Dreams

The traditional Western worldview was that there was a world soul called
the *anima mundi*—the living, dreaming mind of the universe itself. In
these dreams we become entangled with the dream of the Earth, the world
psyche. The indigenous people also had this insight. Currently at the United
Nations there is a global dream initiative called Dreamtending.com.

World dreams immerse us in the vast multidimensional psyche of nature, the Cosmos, where everything is dreaming—every person, creature,
plant, and object is here in this communal realm.[13]

In early November 2020, shortly after the presidential election, I had
this dream:

---

12. David Brooks, "The Floor of Decency."

13. Aizenstat, *Dream Tending.*

> Katy Tur is talking about her despair at the state of the world. She believes that we think that a war would be morally justified. After she has finished, I hear a bomb. I think a war has started.

Katy Tur is a broadcaster on MSNBC. In the dream she is speaking to the anxiety about the state of the world that is felt by many prior to the 2020 U.S. election and the year of COVID-19. I sensed that the world is speaking to me (and many others) to heal the tribal divisions that promote violence and, ultimately, war.

Writing this now on January 20, 2021, after the riots in the Capitol on January 6, I realize that the dream spoke to the deep divisions in the United States.

DREAM TENDING

Keeping an open mind assists you in receiving information from dreams.[14] Allow yourself to move through your dream in a state of "not knowing," allowing yourself the comfort of not having all the answers about the purpose of a dream. Take the dream at face value, without struggling to unravel its knots. Stay open and allow the dream to start informing you.

Dream tending creates an imaginal space, a theater for the dream to enter the waking world. Meet the dream with patience, curiosity, "soft eyes," and deep listening that empties the mind of preconceptions.

A dream image is like a boat moored to a dock. The image reveals itself when it is unmoored and allowed to drift. Rather than interpret a dream, play with images and be attentive to affect and the nuances of the dream, and remain vigilant to the ever-present intrusive presence of ego.

Some practical tips are:

- ❧ Place an open notebook, pen, and flashlight next to your bed. This sets your intention and shows your dreaming psyche that you are dedicated to your dreamlife.

- ❧ Use a gentle alarm clock so you wake up to soft and soothing sounds or music. When you are startled out of sleep, dreams are much more difficult to remember.

---

14. Adapted from Aizenstadt, *Dream Tending*.

- Write down whatever you recall even if it doesn't seem significant. Journaling any dream fragments will also help you remember more dreams.

- Look at the feelings felt by figures in the dream; the feeling tone of the dream is more important than the actual content of the dream. Honestly address the question, "What situation might I be experiencing (or deny experiencing) with feelings similar to those in the dream?"[15]

- Review your dream in that liminal time when you're awake but not out of bed. A voice-activated diary on your phone is immensely helpful when you are half-asleep.

ACTIVE IMAGINATION

For C.G. Jung, Active Imagination was a favorite portal for facilitating an inward journey. In a waking state, a person consciously dialogues with the image of the person or object that has emerged from their unconscious mind and Universal Consciousness.[16]

For example, in an active imagination exercise, a person went through a door and descended to the bottom of a castle. There she had a dialogue with a rock containing a white flame. She had arrived at Universal Consciousness.

JOINING THE DREAMERS

We tend to think that the solution to our problems is in Surface consciousness. But our creative power is our Bedrock consciousness connection to Universal Consciousness, often manifested in dreams.

Our inner process is played out in the outer world. It is an illusion that the two parts of reality—the material world and our inner, subjective world—are separate. A dream is a dialogue between your inner and outer parts of yourself.

The dream needs to impact waking consciousness, to teach the "heroic ego" how to dream and, in doing so, how to experience the world more

15. Hancox, "Dreams are the Royal Road."

16. See Olson, *And God Created Wholeness*, 128–130.

fully. The following dream I had while writing this chapter helped me expand my vision for this work:

> In the midst of creative possibilities, out of a maze of entangled pieces, I designed an orchestra. This book needs to be an original song that will last. Much of it is my shadow and the world's shadow. I cut out some and included others. I am creating rather than repeating the work of others.

In reflecting on the dream, I sensed that it was another world dream. I do feel that in advocating for greater access to Consciousness I am doing work for the world, "that we all may be One." As the lyrics from *Imagine* say:

> "Imagine all the people living life in peace, imagine all the people sharing all the world. You may say I'm a dreamer, but I'm not the only one. I hope someday you'll join us and the world will live as one."[17]

— JOHN LENNON

All spiritual wisdom traditions on this planet have pointed out the dreamlike nature of reality. What if we were to take seriously what these traditions are telling us about the dreamlike nature of our situation? If we interpret experiences in our lives as though we were in a dream, how would this change our experience? What would happen if we continued to explore the Consciousness basis of reality and the power we wield if we connect to Consciousness? How will things change?[18]

Life itself is potentially the dream within which we can become lucid. The more we recognize the dreamlike nature of our waking experience, the more our waking life will reflect this realization and manifest itself in a dreamlike way, thereby increasing our lucidity even further.[19]

Can we collectively embrace the power of open-ended lucid dreaming so as to dream into physical reality the many as-yet-unrealized yearnings that lie deep within us and Consciousness?[20]

---

17. John Winston Lennon, *Imagine* lyrics © Downtown Music Publishing. LyricFind.

18. Adapted from Levy, *The Quantum Revelation*, 303–306.

19. Adapted from Levy, *The Quantum Revelation*, 303–306.

20. Adapted from Levy, *The Quantum Revelation*, 303–306.

Reader Reflection: As you take in the message from the lyrics of Imagine and the power of lucid dreaming, how deep is your resolve to join the world of dreamers?

If your dreams are too elusive for you at this time, *Chapter 6: Waking Portals to Consciousness* has many other accessible portals to Consciousness.

Chapter 6

WAKING PORTALS TO CONSCIOUSNESS

Reader Reflection: What symbol, words, story, ritual, or sound has been especially meaningful or powerful for you? Why is that the case?

OPENING THE DOOR TO CONSCIOUSNESS

IN ADDITION TO OUR DREAMS, we can have a direct experience with Consciousness through any number of spiritual portals. Each personality type can choose their own favorite portal to create an environment that maximizes their experience of the extraordinary.

The filter in the brain that allows access to Consciousness can be opened through meditation, prayer, sounds, music, art, stories, psychedelic drugs, or mediums and spiritual communities. A symbol, a word, a compelling story, a ritual, a particular sound, or music can help you leave the ego behind and open the door to Consciousness. There is a theory that Stonehenge was built with special acoustics so the people could attain a higher level of consciousness.[1]

In accessing Consciousness, we do not hear with our ears or see with our eyes. Just sit with no gain in mind, be open to all experience, do not judge, just notice what is happening. Our intuition expands our knowledge through what Eben Alexander calls "knowledge identification"—a

1. Cox, et al. *Using Scale Modelling to Assess the Prehistoric Acoustics of Stonehenge.*

sudden, absolute knowing of something without all the words to put to it.[2] Understanding escapes boundaries of the intellect and resolves paradoxes. A powerful shift of perspective places you where Consciousness has been pointing. Bernardo Kastrup gives this example:

> In my childhood I could see the moon; in my early adulthood I could only see the finger pointing at the moon; but, during that fleeting moment in Cologne Cathedral, my cognition left the firm earth, and *I was on the moon*.[3]

Our modes of knowing through Bedrock consciousness are modes of knowledge identification, open and more vast than the constraints of Surface consciousness. "Trust your gut" and consider the experience of Consciousness as a gift.

Meditation and Reflection

For many people, the most popular waking portals are meditation and reflection. In quiet solitude, these portals expand our intuition and access the creativity, wisdom, and love of Consciousness.

Our minds can think of dozens of excuses to not meditate. We are too busy, or it is not the right place or time. If we look past the illusion of the hectic pace of daily life, we can connect to the potent stillness and potential of Universal Consciousness that is only as far away as our breath.

Meditation can free us from the reactive patterns and emotional fog of our senses "so that the deep structures of consciousness may become the locus of mystical disclosure."[4] Your inner fears are calmed, and your biases are transformed. You observe your body sensations and your mental reactions to the sensations. You connect to the inner presence of Consciousness. This presence might be a person, a symbol, an animal, a small voice, or something else. You can ask your inner Presence, "What is the most important message I need to receive right now?" Remain calm and still and listen from within, from the heart.

A guided meditation can be especially helpful. Many recordings are available on the Internet. A guided meditation takes you on an inner journey to see and experience your own inner world. At any time, the scenes

---

2. Alexander and Newell, *Explore the Near-Death Experience*, Module Four.

3. Kastrup, *More Than Allegory*, 81.

4. Kourie, "Weaving Colorful Threads," 7.

created in your imagination can be revisited without a guide as an extension of your daily waking consciousness.

What has been stirred by meditation might come in the form of an email from a long-lost friend. There might be a symbol or sign that you keep seeing over and over. It might come to you in a dream, in what other people are talking about, or a song that you're hearing at a particular moment.

Prayer

Prayer is a spiritual practice that allows us to experience Consciousness. As a self-conscious act of humility, it opens the heart to the possibility of love and wisdom emerging from the universe. When we embrace what comes to us, we become the answer to our own prayers. Rev. Dr. Robin R. Meyers explains prayer for non-theists:

> If prayer is a transaction, like a long-distance call or a form of communication between humans and a Deity that 'hears' them and chooses a response, then prayer indeed makes no sense. For a non-theist, no one is 'listening' and no one will 'answer.' . . . If prayer is a self-conscious act of humility, . . . then prayer can become to worship what poetry is to the soul. We can model honesty, vulnerability, courage, and a deeper and more profound trust. If we expect an 'answer' to prayer we remain helpless and in need of rescue.[5]

Sounds and Music

Sound energy has a large spectrum of vibrational frequencies. We are all familiar with the many common sounds of ultrasounds, sonograms, sonar, sonic booms, car horns, and high-pitched dog whistles.

Vibrations are processed in the parts of the brain that have evolved over millions of years in primates and humans. There are ancient circuits down in the lower brainstem where differential frequencies from sounds are processed. These primitive circuits have profound effects of liberating our conscious awareness at that very deep level.

5. Meyers, "If There Is No Theistic God Does Prayer Even Make Sense?" Meyers is retired senior minister of Mayflower Congregational UCC Church, Oklahoma City. Author of *Saving God from Religion*.

Some sounds interact with our minds and foster a certain brainwave state and, thus, a specific state of consciousness. Our internal vibrations resemble music; all music intermingles with our internal vibrations. The effects of a single song may be too small to notice, but the cumulative effects can be significant.[6]

Music makes us feel happy or sad, anxious or euphoric, brave, and determined. Chants, anthems, and hymns have been used to get into non-ordinary levels of human consciousness. For example, in yoga sessions the "om" sound is traditionally chanted at the beginning and end. With roots in Hinduism, this mantra is both a sound and a symbol that has a deep meaning.

Only as humans became isolated from the spiritual and embraced a material worldview has music's power and mystique faded. Today, music is mostly viewed as a form of entertainment—a tragic loss to mankind.[7] As we evolve a higher consciousness and connectivity to other energy fields, spiritual music can hasten our journey back home, connecting us to higher realms of existence.[8]

Words

To experience how words can create a mystical experience, look deeply into the picture of a field of daffodils in Figure 8, then read the poem "Daffodils" by Wordsworth.

6. Mattson, *The Lost Waves of Time*, 14.

7. Mattson, *The Lost Waves of Time*, 10.

8. Mattson, *The Lost Waves of Time*, 390.

Figure 8. Field of Daffodils[9]

Ten thousand saw I at a glance,
Tossing their heads in uprightly dance . . .
I gazed—and gazed—but little thought
What wealth the show to me had brought:
For oft, when on my couch I lie
In vacant or in pensive mood,
They flash upon that inward eye
Which is the bliss of solitude;
And then my heart with pleasure fills
And dances with the daffodils.

Reader Reflection: What did you experience when you read this poem?

The poem becomes a portal to the memory of the flowers that has been stored in Consciousness. We experience them again in our brain's workspace. The words create a flow of energy and information between memory in Consciousness and our minds. Everything—no matter how great their mass, or how hard or solid they appear—are ultimately relationships of living energy and patterns of information.

Metaphors are words that are especially powerful because they enable us to understand reality both intellectually and spiritually. For example,

9. Photo by K. Mitch Hodge on Unsplash.

Chet Raymo provides a metaphor that is a twist on the "baby and the bathwater" story. He suggests that "the bathwater" represents the "mind-stretching, jaw-dropping, in-your-face wonder of the universe itself, the Heraclitan mystery that hides in every rainbow, every snowflake, every living cell."[10] This wonder is Bedrock Consciousness, the creativity in the universe that both scientists and mystics regularly encounter.[11]

The "baby" in the bathwater metaphor stands for our Surface consciousness—the "cultural accretions, the anthropomorphisms, misplaced pieties, triumphalism, intolerance toward 'infidels,' supposed miracles, and supernatural imaginings that religious traditions have placed on the mysteries of the universe." The baby also stands for all our Surface material creations—the product of human labor and creation from the agricultural revolution to rockets that travel to the far reaches of our solar system and beyond.

With the metaphor of baby and bathwater, I can readily intuit the connection of Universal Consciousness (the bathwater) and our egos (the baby). We often need to toss out or transform the "baby," but we always need to save the bathwater!

The bathwater of Consciousness generates the wondrous, breath-taking experiences like a field of daffodils we experience in Surface consciousness. We often call these experiences "sacred."

In our stream of Liminal consciousness—that wash of different sensations, feelings, and emotions—there is much that we cannot describe in words. The feelings we have learned to recognize and label are the ones we notice, but if we learn new words, they can help us articulate whole areas of experience we've only dimly noticed.[12]

Tim Lomas at the University of East London identifies language from other cultures that will aid a more precise and nuanced understanding of such feelings as despair and anxiety.[13]

Of all the words he has found so far, Lomas says that he most often finds himself pondering Japanese concepts such as *wabi-sabi* (the acceptance of transience and imperfection). "It speaks to this idea of finding beauty in phenomena that are aged and imperfect," he says. "If we saw the world through those eyes, it could be a different way of engaging in life."

---

10. Raymo, *When God is Gone*.

11. I used Raymo's metaphor to develop my book *Keep the Bathwater!*

12. Robson, "The 'Untranslatable' Emotions." Robson is BBC Future's feature writer.

13. Lomas, *Translating Happiness: A Cross-Cultural Lexicon of Well-Being*.

Other words that Lomas has found that describe the content of Liminal consciousness are:

- *Tarab* (Arabic): A musically induced state of ecstasy or enchantment.

- *Saudade* (Portuguese): A melancholic longing or nostalgia for a person, place, or thing that is far away either spatially or in time; a vague, dreaming wistfulness for phenomena that may not even exist.

- *Sehnsucht* (German): "Life-longings," an intense desire for alternative states and realizations of life, even if they are unattainable.

- *Dadirri* (Australian aboriginal): A deep, spiritual act of reflective and respectful listening.

- *Sukha* (Sanskrit): Genuine, lasting happiness independent of circumstances.

Chanting powerful words such as Divine names can open a connection to Consciousness.

Symbols

Besides words, our Liminal experiences are often triggered by symbols. For example, a lighthouse and a wizard's wand appeared in a dream about tunneling to Consciousness. The wizard's wand suggested the importance of a mystical approach. The lighthouse beacon was a metaphor for my need to share my received wisdom with others.

Symbols evoke deeper meanings of inner experiences of dreams, visions, imaginings, and outer sensory-based experience. Symbols such as the cross, ring, fire, rainbow, and water represent a vast consciousness that reaches beyond the intellect and into the deep levels of consciousness. In various fairy tales and legends, a fish represents something mysterious or awe-inspiring that suddenly emerges from the depths. This numinous image leads us to seek out its spiritual implications.

Jean Piaget demonstrated that people need to use concrete experiences to attach meaning to abstract ideas. At about two to four years of age, children cannot yet manipulate and transform information in a logical way. However, they can think in images and symbols. Children develop imaginary friends in symbolic play such as playing house or having a tea party.[14]

14. Piaget, *A Child's Conception of Space*, 178.

Becoming more fluent in the symbolic nature of reality develops what Carl Jung called "symbolic awareness." As we see our life symbolically, we find a doorway to Bedrock consciousness.

Symbolic awareness is interrelated with many life processes such as the body's recently discovered ability to turn genes on and off, or the massive, and virtually instantaneous, coordination of quadrillions of life processes per second within the human body. These processes cannot be fully explained by DNA pre-programming or by the relatively slow process of neuron signaling.[15]

> Going Forward: How can you pay more attention to meaningful symbols?
> For example:

- Read a book on symbols.

- Collect miniature symbols you come across that intrigue you.

- Look at the symbols you already have. Why do you have them?

- Go for a walk and observe your environment and any symbol that might reach out to you.

Stories

Stories have the attributes of a living thing. They are not entirely dependent on us.

Because the archetypal content of a story exists prior to the telling, the story is independent of the telling. A story's universal truths have a life force of their own. Once told, it becomes a living story to be woven into other stories, depending on the response from the listeners. If the listeners act on the story, or integrate the story into another, the story becomes an actor of sorts along with us.[16]

Short stories that contain powerful metaphors can be especially effective in shifting levels of consciousness. For example, consider this metaphor for conveying the enormity of climate change:

> Imagine that the Martians arrive, hover over our planet, and aim their weather machines at us to create hurricanes and fires, flood our cities, raise the seas, and otherwise generally cause

15. Selbie, *The Physics of God*, 173.
16. Tyler, "Story Aliveness," 66.

destruction. How would we talk about the problem then? If one candidate showed us a plan for creating a new ray gun to defeat the aliens, and the other candidate insisted everything was fine and the alien ships were actually just clouds, who would you vote for?[17]

Reading sacred texts mythically and mystically for their deep wisdom can be transformative for reading the story of our own lives. By moving from the literal and historical context to our emotional experience with the story, and finally to the spiritual level of what it means, we can reach ever deeper levels of meaning.

Rituals

Rituals are about the here and now, feeling rather than knowing, intuiting rather than deducting, in order to access the dimensions, worlds and categories beyond the materialistic.[18] Rituals dissolve control by the ego to facilitate entering deeper states of consciousness if we let the ritual draw us inward toward an experience of wonder and awe.

Rituals provided prehistoric humans with group structure and hierarchy, enabling specialization and progress. Over time, many rituals have become somewhat empty, more ceremonial than ritual. Rituals connect spirituality and the early roots of Consciousness.[19]

Ritual is everywhere in daily life. We all have our habits, quirks, and patterns. We use repetitive practices to ease the mind, concentrate, meditate, focus, express thanks, or escape the world around us. However, rituals can be a means to connect to Consciousness if we pay close attention and tune into the subtle energies that are always present but that often go unrecognized.

With rituals we can access our deeper dimensions, reaching beyond the rational beyond the limits of space and time, and experience the sacredness of daily life.

17. Manjoo, "There Is Only One Existential Threat."
18. Adapted from Sala, *Ritual.*
19. Adapted from Sala, *Ritual.*

Spirit Guides

Mediums and others who develop a relationship with spirit guides experience an inner knowing, feeling, or strong intuition of their presence. These are spiritual beings not bound by the natural laws of this world. Their common goal is to help us align with the love of the Universe, to move our thoughts from fear back to faith, forgiveness, and light. Spirit practitioners claim that if we trust in our own psychic ability, we are able to hear and allow the spirits to lead us to the highest good of truth and compassion.[20]

I have begun to appreciate the reality of spirit guides. While writing this book I had a telephone session with Mark Anthony,[21] a psychic who is featured on national TV and radio shows. Anthony transmitted information from spirits that wanted to communicate with me, including guidance and support from spirits of several close relatives. It was believable, useful, and confirming of the content of this book.

Psychedelic Drugs

Mainstream acceptance of psychedelics took a significant leap forward when the journal *Nature Medicine* published the results of a study conducted with psychedelic-assisted therapy. This study concluded that MDMA (the drug known as Ecstasy and Molly) paired with counseling brought marked relief to patients with severe post-traumatic stress disorder. A *New England Journal of Medicine* study also highlighted the benefits of treating depression with psilocybin, the psychoactive ingredient in magic mushrooms. Many scientists and psychotherapists in the field of psychedelic medicine believe that the U.S. Food and Drug Administration will grant approval for psychoactive compounds to be used therapeutically—as soon as 2023 for MDMA and a year or two later for psilocybin.[22]

---

20. This description of spirit guides is adapted from Bernstein, *Super Attractor*. Bernstein has been featured on Oprah's *SuperSoul Sunday* and appears regularly as an expert on morning TV shows. Deepak Chopra says, "This book explains with elegant simplicity and practical steps how you can be the author of your life story and manifest your deepest desires and cherished dreams."

21. Anthony, *Evidence of Eternity*.

22. Jacobs, "The Psychedelic Revolution Is Coming."

COMBINING PORTALS TO CONSCIOUSNESS

Combining portals can be an enhanced gateway to Consciousness. For example, painting or coloring may guide you into a meditative state more effectively than sitting still and trying to stop the mind. Mandalas (Figure 9) have guided generations of healers, and visionaries to their own sacred wisdom.

Figure 9. Mandalas are tools to help focus the mind[23]

Walking a labyrinth is another ritual found in all religious traditions that can calm the mind and offer spiritual insight. Walking the complicated path of the labyrinth quiets the mind and helps a person to distinguish superficial extraneous thoughts from what emerges from Consciousness.[24]

Parables have connected Christians to Consciousness as they prayed with the Gospel stories and put themselves imaginatively into the stories. Putting oneself imaginatively into the stories and interacting freely is what St. Ignatius called contemplation. I have found that contemplating parables with the aid of symbols has deepened my understanding of Jesus' message.

For example, consider the parable of the Treasure from Matthew 13:44: *The kingdom of heaven is like treasure hidden in a field, which a man*

23. Photo by Manuswath K B on Unsplash.

24. Artress, *Walking a Sacred Path*, 71.

found and covered up; then in his joy he goes and sells all that he has and buys that field.

The setting here presupposes that someone has buried a treasure and later died. The current owner of the field is unaware of its existence. The finder, perhaps a farm laborer, is entitled to it, but is unable to conveniently extract it unless they buy the field.

The Treasure parable challenges us to go "all in," to give our life to what transcends everything. When we find our treasure, we have fully accessed Consciousness. We become aware of a Presence that lives and breathes and dances throughout the universe and in each of us—and in us together, ready to manifest in myriad ways in lives that bring hope and life.

Teilhard de Chardin would call the Treasure the force of Love-energy, the most universal and most mysterious of the cosmic forces that is both the energy of attraction (withoutness) and the energy of transcendence (withinness).

THE MANY PORTALS TO CONSCIOUSNESS

In his 1917 book, *The Idea of the Holy*, Rudolf Otto used the word "numinous" to describe the unique, special feelings the experience of the sacred produced. A numinous feeling is at once awe-inspiring and fascinating. Words fail us in trying to express our astonishment and wonder. We know we have encountered something beyond the ordinary and "out of this world."

Scientists have experiences and observations that are so awesome that many can only say that what they have demonstrated is sacred. A portal has been opened to lift the veil between everyday reality on the Surface level and the reality of Universal Consciousness.

This recognition of a reality beyond the Surface creates deep humility—the recognition that we exist to serve the whole, in its goodness, truth, and beauty.

Being open to the various portals to the numinous even as we navigate the challenges of daily life can help us see through the fears, resentments, pride, greed, and insecurities of the ego. When we are lonely or hurting, we know that a Presence is moving, dancing, breathing, swirling all around us and will guide us to make life choices on Surface issues with the wisdom from Universal Consciousness.

Going Forward: After reading about the various portals to Consciousness, would you like to:

- ✤ Read books that talk about topics that offer such portals, such as books on dreams?

- ✤ Meditate on the portals that are important to you? What do they evoke for you?

- ✤ Engage a close friend in discussion about what portals are important to both of you?

- ✤ Lead a discussion group or workshop at a church or another organization about accessing Consciousness?

When we encounter a portal to take us to Consciousness, we may be in for a wild ride. In *Chapter 7: Moving Between the Dimensions of Consciousness,* I provide some structure for how to contemplate moving deeper into Consciousness.

Chapter 7

MOVING BETWEEN DIMENSIONS OF CONSCIOUSNESS

THE PORTALS TO CONSCIOUSNESS EXIST in all dimensions of our human consciousness, as we discussed in *Chapter 1*: Surface, Liminal (Positive and Negative), and Bedrock. As depicted in *Figure 10*, Universal Consciousness at the center is continuously present and available to us as we move between the human dimensions of consciousness. The Wholeness Model, which shows the connection of the dimensions of human consciousness, is helpful as we explain some of the multiple paths that are available to gain greater wholeness in our lives.

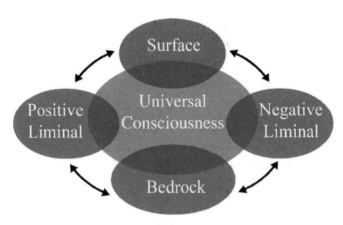

Figure 10. The Wholeness Model of Consciousness[1]

1. Illustration by Tuesday Hadden.

MULTIPLE PATHS TO WHOLENESS

During most of daily life we dwell in Surface consciousness. Our brain seems to need stimulation, so we constantly occupy ourselves with ideas, sensations, entertainment, memories, fantasies, and so on, lest we feel bored.[2]

Every culture has developed technologies, disciplines, and practices to get out of Surface consciousness and access Consciousness. The particular practice and path individuals follow to greater wholeness is influenced by gender, race, age, sexual orientation, religion, mental health, and social/ economic class.

The wide variety of paths are too numerous to include in this chapter, but the paths used by several mystics to move between the dimensions of consciousness illustrate the mystic path to wholeness.

Evelyn Underhill

Evelyn Underhill, an historian of mystical practices, recommends beginning a contemplative journey with the multiplicity of forms in *Surface consciousness*, the natural order of creation.[3] "As to the object of contemplation, . . . anything will do, for all things in this world towards which you are stretching out are linked together, and once truly apprehended will be the gateway to the rest.[4] You transcend consciousness of yourself as you contemplate the song of a bird, the taste of fresh spring water, or a picture of your loved one." Any Surface aspect can give voice to a sacred reality.

In *Liminal consciousness*, "you discover a relationship—far more intimate than anything you imagined—between yourself and the surrounding 'objects of sense.' A subtle interpenetration of your spirit with the spirit of those 'unseen existences,' now so deeply and thrillingly felt by you, will take place. . . . Humility and awe will be evoked in you . . . the experience of sensation without thought."[5]

2. Corbett, *Psyche and the Sacred*, 222.

3. Adapted from Underhill, *Practical Wisdom,* in Olson, *And God Created Wholeness*, 45–71.

4. Adapted from Underhill, *Practical Wisdom,* in Olson, *And God Created Wholeness*, 52.

5. Adapted from Underhill, *Practical Wisdom,* in Olson, *And God Created Wholeness*, 53–55.

In *Bedrock consciousness,* [you] . . . "will find yourself, emptied and freed, in a place stripped bare of all the machinery of thought, and achieve the condition of simplicity. A peculiar certitude which you cannot analyze, a strange satisfaction and peace, is distilled into you."[6]

After the journey through Surface and Liminal contemplation, Underhill says:

> [Now you should] be wisely passive; in order that the great influences which surround you may take and adjust your spirit. . . . let yourself go; cease all conscious, anxious striving and pushing. You must, so far as you are able, give yourself up to, 'die into,' melt into the Whole. [7]

Underhill's final words are inspiring:

> Each new stage achieved in the mystical development of the spirit has meant, not the leaving behind of the previous stages, but an adding on to them: an ever-greater extension of experience, and enrichment of personality. . . . each little event [in your life], each separate demand or invitation which . . . comes to you is now seen in a truer proportion, because you bring to it your awareness of the Whole. . . . Contemplation is not to be for you an end in itself. It shall only be truly yours when it impels you to action. [8]

Underhill says that we must become "a living, ardent tool" of Consciousness, which I discuss in *Chapter 10: Becoming an Agent of Holism.*

Thomas Merton

For Merton, his human condition was a portal to *Bedrock consciousness.* His vulnerability allowed him to deepen intimacy and be in *Liminal consciousness* where everything is divine. It is as if moving through the dimensions of wholeness just happens. A sunset transcends any thoughts. There is a purity of awareness that has a beauty beyond which the *Surface consciousness* can produce.[9]

6. Adapted from Underhill, *Practical Wisdom,* in Olson, *And God Created Wholeness,* 66.

7. Adapted from Underhill, *Practical Wisdom,* in Olson, *And God Created Wholeness,* 72–77.

8. Adapted from Underhill, *Practical Wisdom,* in Olson, *And God Created Wholeness,* 81–88.

9. Adapted from Finley, *Thomas Merton's Path to the Palace of Nowhere.* Finley was a mentee of Merton.

Merton assumed a stance that he was not in control, that he was powerless to achieve, but was aware, attentive, and sustained by Consciousness in his powerlessness. In his contemplative life he was present for the arrival of the sacred. The heightened simplicity of his life gave space for Consciousness to sustain him in all things. He rested in that confidence.

Merton was not focused on outcomes, but on a radical acceptance of what was happening. All life became practice. All of life became a teacher. By learning to listen, Merton learned he was connected to a hidden wholeness where everything connects.

Ilia Delio

Ilia Delio, a renowned theologian who has made major contributions to the integration of science and faith, compares moving between dimensions of consciousness to what occurs in evolution:

> [Evolution] . . . is not repetition of the old world or a cyclic return to the beginning but an ever newness of life born out of the ever newness of love. Divine love is not a river of stagnant water but a fountain fullness of overflowing love, love that is forever awakening to new life. [10]

Delio's description of cycling as a fountain of overflowing love suggests that as we move between the dimensions of Consciousness, we become more whole, more spiritual, and more fully human. We begin to improve how we show up in the world by surrendering and letting go. We stop resisting who and what we truly are and have always been. Our brain's filter is opened to allow the love, peace, and bliss of Universal Consciousness to operate through us without obstruction. Just as each drop of water increases the level of the ocean in a way that we never notice, each individual consciousness that becomes more whole also increases the collective consciousness of our species.

Mirabai Starr

Mirabai Starr, an authority on women mystics, says:

---

10. Delio, *The Unbearable Wholeness of Being,* 77.

> The way of the mystic is the way of surrender, of dying to the false
> self to be reborn as the true Self, the God Self, the radiant, divine
> being we actually are. It's not that the old self—our personality,
> the ego, our stories—is bad or wrong. It's that when we recognize
> the essential emptiness of our individual identity in light of the
> glorious gift of our interconnectedness with the One, indepen-
> dence becomes much less compelling. And that's the path of the
> feminine: the path of connections.[11]

Starr's feminine path suggests that as we develop greater wholeness,
we remain longer in Bedrock consciousness to access Universal Consciousness. The content in Universal Consciousness flickers in and out, overlapping, combining, separating, flowing, in ways we can't quite imagine—ruled
by physical laws we do not yet understand. Numinous images, thoughts,
and feelings arrive from a reality not in our control.[12]

Eben Alexander

Eben Alexander described a divine presence as the "core realm" he encountered in his near-death experience (NDE):

> . . . [I]t all came together there in an infinite, inky blackness that
> had this brilliant orb of light that was there as an interpreter or
> translator. But the thing was so amazing that in spite of this sense
> of infinities and eternities, and that my awareness was now bigger
> than all of that, there was still this sense [of] the love of that divine
> force, that God force of love.[13]

In his discussion of his NDE, Alexander describes a conceptual flow
of a mode of truth that he was loved and cherished forever, that he had
nothing to fear, that we would be taken care of.[14] Like the "flow of truth"
that Alexander experienced, when we move through the dimensions of
Consciousness, there is a flow that enables us to navigate the journey.

Alexander's NDE has a timeless and spaceless quality, but we do not
need an NDE to have "a personal, subjective, here-and-now, one-of-a-kind
encounter with, and immersion in, the source and essence of mystical

---

11. Starr, *Wild Mercy,* 67.

12. Hansen, *Neurodharma,* 217.

13. Alexander and Newell, *Explore the Near-Death Experience,* Module Six.

14. Alexander and Newell, *Explore the Near-Death Experience,* Module Four.

consciousness at any time."[15] Unexplainable and unpredictable coincidences may arise at any time—in dreams but also in moments of crisis, moments of relaxation (e.g., while in the shower), or when we actively try to engage deeper levels of consciousness.

Hindu Seers

For Hindu seers, the "Akasha" is the fundamental dimension, existing prior to the observed dimensions of the four elements of air, fire, water, and earth. The world is a cyclic presence, emerging from, and falling back into, the Akasha, the Whole.[16]

Like Akasha, in a time of uncertainty, our Bedrock consciousness provides solid ground. When our personal attachments and institutions that have given us security, happiness and love have failed, we can find peace and joy in Universal Consciousness.[17] We can think of despair as a gift, a dark night of the soul of desperation that brings a challenge to our old worldview, our old beliefs, so that we can open up to a better world—a kinder, gentler more cohesive world. Pay attention to what is happening in Liminal consciousness and enter into the Bedrock to connect to Universal Consciousness where we know that all will be well.

Edwin E. Olson

In my encounters with Universal Consciousness, I have felt exhilarated by a powerful sense of connectedness, a oneness with the world and its peoples. I still remember the vision I had of my grandmother Margaret Halsrud when staying in her home shortly after her death. I was overcome by a sense that all was well as she affirmed me with her presence. Words fail to adequately describe the experience.

In accessing Universal Consciousness, I agree with Mark Gober that "a surrendered attitude toward knowledge might have the benefit of allowing us to absorb more of the One Mind's intelligence."[18] Adopting an attitude of

---

15. Robinson, *Mystical Activism*, 55. Robinson is a clinical psychologist and an ordained interfaith minister.

16. Laszlo, *Reconnecting to the Source*, 13; Laszlo, *New Science for a New World*.

17. Spira, *The Nature of Consciousness*.

18. Gober, *An End to Upside Down Living*, 87.

surrender involves loving myself enough to quiet the inner voice, to quell distracting thoughts, and detach from Surface consciousness.

My favorite mythical metaphor about moving through the dimensions of consciousness, perhaps because my father was Finnish, is the story of the hero Väinämöinen in the Finnish epic of Kalevala. He wounded his leg with an axe while cutting a tree (Surface consciousness). The wound would not heal so he began a journey to find the origin of the axe blade and handle—the instrument that wounded him. By going deep into the origin of things, he entered Bedrock consciousness where there is a dynamic, healing potential that is always active because of its connection to Universal Consciousness.

I also like the metaphor that Universal Consciousness is the magnetism that creates coherence in Bedrock consciousness, analogous to the powerful magnets in an MRI machine that turn on and off in a series of quick pulses, causing each hydrogen atom to change its alignment when switched on and then quickly switch back to its original relaxed state when switched off. This magnetism is not a controlling force, but it has a profound effect on my life. The presence has the soft qualities of love, vulnerability, and forgiveness. Those forces are inherently indeterminate in the sense that they cannot force any particular outcome. When I surrender to this magnetic presence, I trust that it is acting in my best interest.

APPLICATION OF THE WHOLENESS MODEL
TO THE MYSTICAL PATH

Our world views and interpretations of events inevitably become fossilized and non-adaptive if we view life through only our Surface consciousness. By moving between the dimensions, we can create conditions for something new to emerge. We can see the deep connectedness between ourselves and others, and develop compassion as we become still and listen.

Movement between the dimensions of consciousness is generally a progressive spiral to greater consciousness and wholeness. When we have positive outcomes from meditation or prayer in Bedrock consciousness, we are moved to Liminal-Positive consciousness, where we experience joy and the energy to return to Surface consciousness to deal with our issues, enlightened by our experience in Liminal consciousness. We access Bedrock consciousness to intuit creative possibilities, and connect to the wisdom and love from Universal Consciousness.

It can also be a retrogressive spiral that doesn't move us along a path to wholeness.

For example, when we have issues and concerns in Surface consciousness, we then move to Liminal-Negative consciousness where there is a turbulence of images, feelings, and thoughts about what we should do. We may just move back and forth between Surface and Liminal as we piece together plans, solutions, and next steps.

If you are in a bad mood (Liminal-Negative), you may return to Surface consciousness to muddle through your daily life, ruminate about the problem, and continue to move back and forth between Surface and Liminal-Negative. Or you may decide to calm down, meditate and go to Bedrock consciousness.

All mystics experienced an emotional state between contemplation and action. This is reflected in the Wholeness Model. Movement between Surface and Bedrock consciousness always goes through Liminal consciousness, positive or negative.

Moving between the dimensions physically hardwires our brain as we build dedicated circuitry for the choices we make in life. We can choose paths that only enhance our ego. Or we can choose the paths that are of service to others and the world.[19] Who we are, our identity, is what emerges from the process.

Aldous Huxley wrote that we need to access the mystical experiences of Consciousness, what he called the "Mind-at-Large," for our survival:

> To make biological survival possible, Mind-at-Large must be funneled through the reducing valve of the brain and nervous system. What comes out at the other end is a measly trickle of the kind of consciousness that would help us stay alive on the surface of this planet.[20]

Hopefully, learning more about Consciousness will help all of us to "stay alive on the surface of this planet" as Huxley hoped.

Reader Reflection: Who have you read or been influenced by who models how you can move between the dimensions of consciousness in your daily life?

19. Hollis, *Finding Meaning in the Second Half of Life*, 189.
20. Huxley, *The Doors of Perception*.

As we move between the dimensions of consciousness, we encounter what is commonly called "our shadow,"[21] aspects of our self of which we are unaware, want to avoid, fear, deny, or project onto others. In *Part III: Toward Greater Wholeness,* we see how dealing with our individual and collective shadows is essential for progression toward greater wholeness.

---

21. Along with "shadow" there are usually references to dark, even black, to identify what is considered to be fearful or disgusting. To not perpetuate terms with racist implications, I will only use the term "shadow."

Part II Implications

DISCOVERING WHAT IS REAL

EXPERIENCING WHOLENESS

DURING OUR ISOLATION IN THE COVID-19 pandemic, many of us have experienced the silent world of wholeness, a non-dual oneness. But then we step out into the world where separateness dominates. Only a consciousness of wholeness at every level—personal, interpersonal, cultural, political, and spiritual—can overcome our tribal divisions.

Jesus uses the phrase "the kingdom of heaven" to indicate the kingdom within us and the kingdom that is at hand. This is a metaphor for the state of Consciousness—not a place we go to but a place we come from. It is transformed awareness that literally turns this world into a different place. There is no separation between Consciousness and humans, nor between one human and another human. When Jesus talks about this oneness, he means a complete, mutual indwelling.[1]

CONSCIOUSNESS IS INCLUSIVE

The Consciousness paradigm enables people from all faiths and secular traditions to connect to the Source that unites us, including our earth in love, caring, and affection.[2]

---

1. Bourgeault, *The Wisdom Jesus*, 30–32.
2. Dossey, *One Mind*.

If we acknowledge that self-creation and Consciousness are fundamental, we can develop a shared vision that would foster well-being at every level. This is how social change can happen. If we have a shared intention, we have a powerful force for change—a worldview, not a technology.[3]

Everything we see, touch, hear, taste, smell, and imagine is a potential portal to Universal Consciousness.

The Consciousness paradigm provides non-dualistic language that is evolutionary, coherent, and anticipatory of the future, liberating us from any fixed problems of the past. Consciousness includes both life and death, which allow our story to unfold. The universe isn't pointless because the story is continuing. Christians may regard embracing the Consciousness paradigm as taking on a "Christ Consciousness."

Many spiritual giants of all religions like St. Francis, Julian of Norwich, Dorothy Day, and Mohandas Gandhi tried to live their entire lives in the permanent liminality of Consciousness, on the edge or periphery of the dominant culture. They valued silence, experiencing emptiness, anonymity, and pennilessness. From this space they reentered the world with freedom and new creative approaches to life.[4]

CONNECTING TO WHOLENESS

Younger generations who are looking for existential purpose will not find it in consumerism and careerism. Greater awareness of what is of ultimate concern will draw them into communities of like-minded people to explore what is of ultimate value. As they connect to Universal Consciousness, the value of their relationships with all aspects of planetary life will become clear.

Transitioning to a sustained connection to Consciousness may require several generations. Fully accessing Consciousness will require becoming a mystic, not a solitary individual living in a cave, but an *active mystic*,[5] fully engaged in the moral, social, economic, and political issues of the world.

> The only path forward for the survival of our species, and perhaps even our planet, is a path of nonviolence, of contemplation and action prioritizing justice and solidarity, an affirmation of Oneness

3. Schwartz, *The Transformation*.

4. Adapted from Rohr, *Adam's Return*, 135–138.

5. Robinson, *Mystical Activism*.

and the interconnectedness of all things, which science confirms, and spirituality has always known on its deepest level.[6]

DISCOVERING WHAT IS REAL

We discover what is real by moving through the dimensions of Consciousness—Surface consciousness (self-awareness), Liminal consciousness (imaginal reality), and Bedrock consciousness (deep intuition)—which connects us to Universal Consciousness of wisdom and unconditional love. In Bedrock consciousness, we encounter the Presence that holds and sustains us in a time of hope and lament. Maintaining a mystical perspective, we are less likely to get caught up in a cycle of rumination between our Liminal and Surface consciousness that is not life-sustaining.

As I become more aware of the intelligence in the diverse mystical paths that are all around me, I see things differently. I see how things have developed in history. I see the gradual change between the seasons and the marvel of birds building their nests. I see the significant difference between my life and the lives of Black, Indigenous, and People of Color (BIPOC). I see connections and synchronicities.

As I create an imaginal space, I allow Universal Consciousness to enter. I suppress my belief in materialism and see my intelligence as a subset of the intelligence in the Universe.

I become a different person. I connect to an inner stillness and an experience that liberates me from the demands of my ego. I become more creative in how to live and love and build community. I move into a deeper story about who I am. I am saved from my previous narrow self-identity.

I see the wholes that are greater than their parts. I open new portals to Consciousness and see what the collective consciousness wants me to do with my life. I am challenged to wonder what benefit I provide to the Earth.

6. Rohr, *The Freedom of Consent*, blog, October 30, 2020.

Part III

TOWARD GREATER WHOLENESS

"There is in all visible things an invisible fecundity, a dimmed light, a meek namelessness, a hidden whole-ness. This mysterious Unity and Integrity is Wisdom, the Mother of all, *Natura naturans*.[1] There is in all things an inexhaustible sweetness and purity, a silence that is a fount of action and joy. It rises up in word-less gentleness and flows out to me from the unseen roots of all created being, welcoming me tenderly, saluting me with indescribable humility."[2]

—THOMAS MERTON

INTRODUCTION: WHOLENESS AS OMEGA

WHEN WE ACCESS THE THREE dimensions of Consciousness, we develop our larger Self, our subjective inner life, our conscious experience of the sensations of our body, our feelings, and our thoughts. We access the inner wholeness described by Merton. We access the wisdom and unconditional love of Universal Consciousness and develop a sense of being whole, a part of an indivisible Oneness.

Teilhard de Chardin explained that evolution in our unfinished universe is not chaotic and random, but convergent toward what he called the *Omega Point*—a force of infinite love that guides our paths and teaches us that we are all integral parts of a greater wholeness. Chardin theorized that

1. A Latin term coined during the Middle Ages, meaning "Nature naturing," or more loosely, "nature doing what nature does."
2. Pramuk, in *Sophia*.

79

the progressive growth of consciousness itself is ultimately the purpose of our existence.[3]

Chardin also coined the term *noosphere* to describe an emergent collective level of unity consciousness, a super intelligence infusing all of us with trans-human awareness and intelligence. The development of a noosphere in which artificial mental boundaries will be erased will likely be aided by technology, especially Artificial Intelligence (A.I.).

Spiritual growth begins with an intuition of the wholeness that is possible for us. Our highest happiness comes from being of service to the Whole, in its goodness, truth, and beauty.[4] "Wholeness does not mean perfection: it means embracing brokenness as an integral part of life."[5]

Life in our Surface existence creates "karma," our distinctive patterns and behavioral tendencies which, over time, become our personalities, our sense of self.[6] To get out of any destructive patterns and behaviors we need to go to Bedrock consciousness. With our connection to Universal Consciousness, we are linked to our true Self and the rest of the world. We need to go deep to find the wisdom to engage our Surface challenges. Matthew Fox puts it this way:

> We need to go down deep into the darkness, into the mystery, into the shadow, into the forgotten parts of ourselves as individuals and communities and as a species. We must also come back to the surface changed and ready to make change. The future requires all of us to dive deep and return, surfacing with the wisdom, the mysteries, and the truths we learned from diving.[7]

Instead of diving deep as Matthew Fox urges, in 2020 our individual and collective fear and stress broke that wholeness for many, and ultimately many souls became sick and died. We were in a "global dark night" of global warming, pandemics, species extinction, and rampant capitalism of greed.[8]

The January 6, 2021, insurrection on the U.S. Capitol, when many were caught up in a collective narcissism, was the reality of evil. Hopefully, in the months afterward and beyond, we will be awakened and become conscious of the Whole. Fox put our hoped-for awakening this way:

3. Savary, *Teilhard de Chardin's The Phenomenon of Man*, 132.

4. Patton, *A New Republic of the Heart*, 179.

5. Palmer, *A Hidden Wholeness*.

6. Sadhguru, *Karma*.

7. Fox, *Meister Eckhart*, 274–275.

8. Harvey and Baker, *Radical Regeneration*.

. . . Today, thanks to the women's movement, the ecology movement, the Black Lives Matter movement, and to the facts of climate
change and its child, the coronavirus, we are awakening to what
we have done—and the price we have paid.[9]

Perhaps we were not ready to hear the wholeness message from Consciousness. Perhaps we are now ready to confront the source of our racism, our antiquated view of personhood. Perhaps we are now ready for the
wisdom of the mystics like Julian of Norwich. Julian was fully aware of the
plague that afflicted her generation, but she didn't go to a dark place. She
affirmed a democracy of justice and caring, unity, trust, cooperation, the
web of creation, joy, and a healthy self-love and service to others.[10]

In *Chapter 8: Personal Wholeness*, we consider how, as individuals, we
can progress toward greater wholeness by confronting our unique shadows.
In *Chapter 9: Collective Wholeness*, we consider the larger collective shadow
to which we are contributing and that is controlling our individual lives.
When we see the collective underlying shadow, we can focus our social activism for the greater good. In *Chapter 10: Becoming an Agent of Holism*, we
consider what is involved in becoming a proponent and an agent of holism
to restore wholeness (should we decide to accept the mission).[11]

9. Fox, *Julian of Norwich*, 111.

10. Fox, *Julian of Norwich*, 124.

11. Think of Tom Cruise accepting a "Mission Impossible." He succeeds because he
has a great team. Your team is comprised of all of your considerable strengths.

Chapter 8

PERSONAL WHOLENESS

WHOLENESS IS OUR DEEPEST IDENTITY. We become a whole *person* when we recognize our connection to the wider field of life and when we open the boundaries that keep us from moving toward others.

When we identify as an *individual,* we see ourselves as different from the whole. The more unique I think I am, the more I am locked into the reality I have constructed for myself.

Personhood is a constructive process of ongoing identity. Ilia Delio likens this ongoing dynamical process to the "self," a mini expanding universe open to life.[1]

I had a dream several years ago in which these statements appeared: "Truthing is a process like Selfing" and "The problem with morals and values is the absolute nature of the dialogue." I believe the message from the dream is that becoming a "Self" is not a process of learning absolutes. "Selfing" is like the dynamical process of searching for truth. The Self, as well as the Truth, emerges from the Whole as we converge with the "Other"—our shadow and people who are different from us.

We become a whole person when we soften the boundaries of our individual identity, become fully open to life, and join the greater Whole.

> *Reader Reflection: Complete this statement: "I am" . . . Repeat it several times. What self-identities come up? Which identities do you think about most often?*

Will we grow into personhood by accessing Consciousness and our relationship to the Whole? Will we strengthen our desire, hope, and longing

---

1. Delio, *Hours of the Universe,* 113.

for the possibilities that Wholeness offers? This chapter is about how connecting to Universal Consciousness can transform self-identities, integrate shadows, develop greater wholeness, and flourish in a technological world.

THE STORY WE CREATE

Without a connection to Consciousness, our identity and the story we manufacture and update about ourselves is fictional.[2]

Yuval Harari describes the storyteller in our minds that explains who we are, where we come from, where we are heading, and what is happening to us right now. This inner narrator repeatedly gets things wrong but rarely admits it. Our inner propaganda machine creates a personal myth with prized memories and cherished traumas that often bear little resemblance to the truth.[3] He says:

> . . . 99 percent of what we experience never becomes part of the story of the self. A family holiday fraught with traffic jams, petty squabbles, intense silences become a collection of beautiful panoramas, perfect dinners, and smiling faces.[4]

The story created by our ego lets us navigate in the world around us but, as long as the ego is on autopilot, we go through daily life mechanically, without full awareness of what we are doing. We are encouraged to focus outward in Surface waking consciousness. An avalanche of advertising implies that happiness is about consuming more or being entertained. We are also directed outward by constant warnings about the presence of enemies.

In the process, our ego separates us from one another, obscuring the reality that no such separation exists. Our cultural attitudes rarely promote much introspection or self-reflection about who we really are.

A big part of the story about ourselves is about our expectations, which others have put on us or we have created to further the aims of our ego. Unfulfilled expectations yield resentments.

Richard Rohr says that to change or let go of our egocentric preoccupations and expectations, we must "lose" at something. Any conscious attempt to engineer or plan our own enlightenment is doomed to failure because it will be ego driven. We will try to "succeed" in the midst of our

---

2. Laszlo, *Reconnecting to the Source*, 35.
3. Harari, 21 *Lessons for the 21st Century*, 307.
4. Harari, 21 *Lessons for the 21st Century*, 307.

failure, but we stumble and are brought to our knees by reality. Some kind of "necessary suffering" is programmed into the journey.[5] By avoiding our shadow, many of us have kept ourselves from our own spiritual depths.

WHAT IS THE SHADOW?

The shadow is a part of our psyche (mind) that comes to us in the service of wholeness, including negative feelings and emotions that have been repressed and kept unconscious. It is the part of ourselves we do not want to acknowledge. It could be our selfishness, greed, envy, or anger, but it also could be positive qualities we fear. For example, a person with low self-esteem may not be in touch with his or her talents. These positive qualities are in that person's shadow, just as the habitual criminal has an impulse to be law-abiding.[6]

> *Reader Reflection: Carl Jung said that what you are unaware of (your shadow) will direct your life. What aspects of your personality do you dislike and are even ashamed of when they pop up? Be honest about this. It will be helpful even if a bit frightening or embarrassing.*

Unless we face our shadow, we will feel continually trapped in the same thoughts and behaviors. Asking friends and loved ones to provide honest feedback about our blind spots can be helpful. Shining a light on our shadow provides a deeper sense of the Self.

The shadow can be observed during arguments and when a person is intoxicated or otherwise not in control. When expressed, a person may say, "I'm so sorry; I didn't mean that. That is not me." In dreams, the shadow is often seen as figures behaving in ways that our conscious mind would repudiate.

We heal others as well as ourselves by bringing our shadow into our Surface consciousness. When we acknowledge our shadow, we acknowledge that we are not perfect. If we experience the negative emotions of the shadow and allow those feelings to exist, we are confronting our core issues. Dealing with shadow issues allows us to integrate them into who we are and get to that state of pure awareness of Consciousness. The shadow loses its power. It may even become a source of amusement.

---

5. Adapted from Rohr, *Falling Upward*, xix–xx, 65–66, 68.

6. Corbett, *Psyche and the Sacred*, 162.

Yoram Inspector, a Jungian analyst in New York City, tells this story about a person being befriended by his shadow: An Auschwitz survivor couldn't sleep because of his painful memories but then had a dream that he was a Nazi officer. When he woke, he realized that if he had been raised in Germany, he could have been that Nazi officer. He was then able to sleep.

When I am befriended by my shadow, I can be authentic and not project my shadow on others. For example, I have had to change and let go of my white supremacy. As I have seen and experienced systemic racism and oppression, I realized I have stopped myself from reaching out. I have remained silent. I saw discrimination and did not speak. I remained on the margin, choosing to be helpless, rather than confront the issues.

I have learned to use my white privilege to better serve others. I can let go of being competent and be vulnerable to join others in their pain. I do not need to control the situation or its outcome. I can confront my fellow white males in a timely fashion. My learning about and encountering my shadow is a continuous process as I learn more about how power is assigned and distributed in our culture. For example, I recently attended a Zoom meeting of a mixed-race group of educators. Here is what happened:

> A white colleague of mine ('Sam') compared the discrimination he suffered as a child with red hair to the life-long suffering of a black colleague ('Rhonda') who has experienced systemic racism. When Rhonda told Sam that she felt diminished when she heard that comparison, Sam felt hurt. He felt he could not express his reality as a child and was 'doing it wrong.' I initially was caught up with empathy for Sam's story. I trusted Sam's ability to sort out and resolve his issue. I thought others in the group would intervene. I was reluctant to confront Sam while he was in pain.

After the group meeting, I reflected that I could have asked Sam if what he was feeling could be his way of maintaining control—that he was interacting in a way that suited him but was not okay for others. I could have created space for Sam to reflect on using his white privilege in the mixed-race group.

Holding onto and exhibiting his hurt was a means of maintaining white superiority in the group. Sam wanted to be accepted as he is. Being uncomfortable in a mixed-race group is a white weapon. Sam exercised power but acted disempowered.

I and all whites need to let go of habits and behaviors that serve to maintain control of other races and instead strive for shared control and power. One of my other white female colleagues said this about her awakening:

> I allow my principles to blind me as to the impact on people of color. I insist on following the rules, but these rules are biased in favor of the dominant society. I have a set of values that can be discriminatory. As a member of the dominant society, I have to ask: What am I prepared to give up?

Giving up privilege and using privilege are two different things. Using it to "improve" the behavior of others casts doubt that they could do it themselves. Giving up privilege is about recognizing privilege and then making room—making your privilege smaller so other people have room.

When we integrate our shadow, we can use the energy from it with awareness. Recognize it and then choose what to do with it. My shadow is the smokiness between our two mirrors. It keeps me from seeing you.

Reader Reflection: What privilege are you willing to give up in order to open more possibilities and agency for others?

OUR TRUE SELF

Doing our shadow work on all of the 'isms is the work of changing from a smaller and constricted self to a larger, more open Self that accesses Consciousness. We must deal with the myriad tasks and worries in our daily life, but if they dominate our thinking, we miss the larger task of connecting to the wholeness of Consciousness.

Richard Rohr calls the small self the "False Self," the self we manufacture and adopt to find our identity in the world. False doesn't mean that it's bad; it means that it is external and is influenced by conventional wisdom. Everyone has a False Self to function in the world.

Rohr calls the larger Self the "True Self," our innermost, essential being.[7] Our True Self is not our ego; we find our True Self in our connection to Consciousness. When we meditate, we find our Self that is filtered out by the brain (see *Chapter 2*).

John Duns Scotus (1266–1308) said that the human person is not different or separate from Being itself—Universal Being.[8] Thomas Merton

---

7. Rohr, *Immortal Diamond*.
8. Rohr, "True Self/Separate Self," blog, August 30, 2020.

identified the True Self with life itself,[9] but not the small self of our ego and persona in Surface consciousness. Merton's classic description of the True Self was written following his "conversion" at Fourth and Walnut in Louisville, Kentucky:

> At the center of our being is a point of nothingness . . . a point of pure truth . . . It is like a pure diamond. It is in everybody, and if we could see it, we would see these billions of points of light coming together in the face and blaze of a sun that would make all the darkness and cruelty of life vanish completely.[10]

Richard Rohr describes our tendency to identify Life with our small self:

> When you've gotten too comfortable with your separate self and you call it Life, you will get trapped at that [Surface] level. You will hold onto it for dear life—because that's the only life you think you have! Unless someone tells you about the Bigger Life, or you've had a conscious connection with the deepest ground of your being, there's no way you're going to let go of your separate self. Your True Self is Life and Being and Love. Love is what you were made for and love is who you are. When you live outside of Love, you are not living from your true Being or with full consciousness.[11]

ARTIFICIAL INTELLIGENCE (A.I.)

The technology of the printing press created an unpredictable outcome. It changed the way we gather information and think. We don't know what will happen with new technology. We need to be prepared for impacts on our cultural ethics, including the impact of psychedelic drugs. What will be the impact of putting a chip in a person? What will it do to your brain? The Internet is already an extension of our memory, aiding our brain as an external hard drive so we don't need to remember as many facts.

Technology has become an existential imperative in our Surface consciousness. Upon waking, many of us feel compelled to immediately check websites, emails, Twitter, Facebook, and Instagram, etc. Our alternate lives are a mere click away, keeping us tethered to our devices.

9. Merton, *New Seeds of Contemplation.*

10. Merton, *Conjectures of a Guilty Bystander*, 142.

11. Adapted from Rohr, *True Self/False Self.*

Artificial intelligence will be able to unlock our inner wizard by artificially inducing brain states that enable on-demand psychic abilities. The brain is a tool to access the memories; memories stream from Universal Consciousness and are not stored in the brain. "Certain parts of the brain might be related to the memory access process, but they don't house the memories."[12] How might A.I. enable greater access to these memories?

Consciousness can provide a framework and structure to expand the mystical dimension of life using technology and A.I. to extend our biological intelligence. There will be new "apps for the mind." We can express our insights, visions, and imagination in new ways. Much of the current technology immerses us in the world of entertainment, politics, and consumerism that does not lead us to wholeness but, rather, to a lack of meaning and harmful fragmentation. The challenge will be to partake of these technologies so they take us to higher states of consciousness.

TOWARD GREATER PERSONAL WHOLENESS

As we become more whole, we navigate our life with more wisdom. We can more clearly assess our life situations. We can step into new possibilities with more confidence. We feel more joy, empowerment, and gratitude. We can ride the waves of change more gracefully. Carl Jung understood "that we are ultimately grounded in something infinite and eternal, and that our lives as finite beings, illusory as they may be, serve a divine purpose."[13] The guidance and support from Consciousness improves our health and well-being, and enable us to be in service to the planet.

As far as we know, we represent the highest level of self-reflective consciousness in the universe and the most intense physical being open to Universal Consciousness. Ilia Delio says:

> These characteristics do not set humans apart from the earth but rather as the living expression of earth's potential for more life. We have the capacity to think the earth into greater wholeness and to live on a new level of complexity consciousness. Insights from modern science help us realize that with the emergence of the modern human person, the universe becomes a self-reflective universe.[14]

12. Gober, *An End to Upside Down Living*, 70.

13. Kastrup, *Decoding Jung's Metaphysics*, 115.

14. Delio, *Re-Enchanting the Earth*, 26.

Here are some ways to be more self-reflective and increase personal wholeness:

- ⤙ Immerse yourself in nature (Figure 11) and appreciate the wonder of our rivers, the ocean, the birds, the trees, clouds, the hills and mountains; and marvel at the transition from one season to another.

- ⤙ Recognize the little miracles of ordinary events and interactions, beginning with the awareness that there is an abundant supply of air for your breath.

- ⤙ Join a mindfulness or dialogue group.

- ⤙ Use Centering prayer to rewire your neurons so you can let go of anxiety and control of things you can't do anything about.

- ⤙ Join awareness-raising movements that work to resolve issues in health, education, climate change, business, and politics.

- ⤙ Choose to be a spiritual leader or a social and political activist.

- ⤙ Sit still and enjoy your surroundings.

Figure 11. Immersing yourself in nature can be as simple as taking a walk[15]

The work of integrating the shadow is made more difficult by the fact that our personal shadow also contains the shadow aspects of the culture in which we live, with its violence, prejudices, and indifference to social injustice. If only by our silence, we participate in the shadow that is around us.

15. Photo by Melinda Thiessen Spencer.

We can awaken to our true and whole Self as we face this collective shadow in *Chapter 9: Collective Wholeness.*[16] We can assimilate the knowledge and power of our shadow in our unconditional desire to know and periodically re-examine who we are and what is the truth ("Selfing and Truthing").

16. Bates, *Pigs Eat Wolves*, 89.

Chapter 9

COLLECTIVE WHOLENESS

IN *PART II*, WE IDENTIFIED portals to Consciousness and discussed how entering these portals and moving through the dimensions of Consciousness create greater wholeness. We applied the Wholeness Model to developing individual wholeness in *Chapter 8: Personal Wholeness* by integrating our personal shadow so our True Self can emerge. In this chapter, we explore how to develop the collective Wholeness we need to transform the Anthropocene.

OUR COLLECTIVE CRISES

I wrote the first draft of this chapter on June 2, 2020, at the height of the demonstrations and riots set off by the death of George Floyd at the knee of a policeman in Minneapolis. The nation was also coping with the COVID-19 worldwide pandemic, which killed over 700,000 people in the United States by late 2021 and is still killing.

Our current existential crises are revealing our collective shadow of 'isms: racism, sexism, ageism, classism, and other cultural demographics that separate us into warring tribes. "Me-ism" is also evident in the resistance to wearing a mask to prevent exposing others to the COVID-19 virus and a rush to open the economy without sufficient regard for public safety.

Regarding the grievances of Black, Indigenous, and People of Color (BIPOC), many are searching for band-aids. Many whites just want the conflict to go away, by any means. White supremacy and patriarchy support racism and sexism with power dynamics and covert processes. The dominant groups in any society always exercise power. The question is: Is that exercise of power for the public good—the good of all—or is it serving the narrow self-interest of the dominant class and maintaining our political divide?

Our human-made crises stem from our collective shadow.

WHAT IS THE COLLECTIVE SHADOW?

The collective shadow is an invisible but very real and powerful energy force made up of every individual's shadow. Imagine this as the force inside a volcano. The volcano is in a mountain above the ground that we can all see, but there is a growing pressure of bubbling lava inside the mountain. Most of the population are oblivious to its existence, going about their daily lives around the mountain with no awareness of what is inside and what is about to occur.

As with an individual shadow, this collective shadow can stay buried for a long time, but sooner or later, either the shadow contents become too massive for the societal structures to contain, or a trigger cracks societal structures and the shadow emerges—often extremely fast—and 'projects' itself onto something or someone outside of itself. It can be projected upon a person, a partner, a group, a political party, a religion, an entire race of people, a species of animal, women, men, a company, an accident, an event, or even a virus: anything can receive the projection of the shadow.

Groups, organizations, institutions, and nations have shadows that manifest as fear, panic, destruction, confinement, isolation, depression, loss of meaning and purpose, and pain and death to others. Over time, the pressure to face these concerns bubbles up until a spark brings them to our collective attention. When these manifestations are encountered, the usual impulse is to cover them up as soon as possible so the collective Surface consciousness is disturbed as little as possible.

The projection of the collective shadow is at the root of wars, witch burnings, genocide, *pogroms*, crusades, and many massacres of "heretics."[1]

Included in the collective shadow of the United States is materialism, which breeds overconsumption, valuing property over people, and valuing individual rights over the rights of the whole. Many Americans refuse to

---

1. Corbett, *Psyche and the Sacred*, 145.

value the social whole (what's best for the community, the public good). Each of us thinks we know what's best for ourselves.[2]

National cohesion, sacrifice for the common good, and trust in each other and our institutions is sorely lacking.

Perhaps because of their focus on their own material well-being, when the Capitol was besieged on January 6, 2021, many Americans were shocked about the prevalence of election denialism, anti-science beliefs, white supremacy, and anti-democratic and even fascist-leaning sentiments in the country.

UNAWARENESS OF SHADOW

When a large swath of humanity cannot, does not, or is afraid to observe their own minds, the shadow is present. Whenever a group, society, or nation becomes too preoccupied with ensuring their survival, they develop a strong shadow, believing in their own preeminence, superiority, and entitlement.

Others do not want to look at their own motivations because they might see something they would have to change, which takes effort. So, they adopt views of themselves that do not require self-examination. "I am just fine the way I am." "My problems are caused by other people. I am a victim." "Other people's problems are not my problem." "I'm responsible for only myself and my family."

Many sensitive people do feel the existence of the collective shadow. Many had insights and dreams that something big was coming in 2021. Those attuned to the changing climate and environment know that we are reaching a tipping point, or had reached it some time ago, and were now at a cracking point.

Awareness of the contents of your own shadow is vital to understanding and weakening our collective shadow. Jung said:

> The psychology of the individual is reflected in the psychology of the nation. What the nation does is done also by each individual, and so long as the individual continues to do it, the nation will do

2. Damon Linker quoted in David Brooks, "The National Humiliation We Need," A23. Brooks drives home the point with this remark: "If you don't breathe the spirit of the nation, if you don't have a fierce sense of belonging to each other, you're not going to sacrifice for the common good. We're confronted with a succession of wicked problems, and it turns out we're not even capable of putting on a friggin' mask."

likewise. Only a change in the attitude of the individual can initiate a change in the psychology of the nation.[3]

Contributing to the lack of awareness is our current spate of misinformation and outright disinformation. The cultural climate is ripe to make people susceptible to believing and sharing misinformation. Protecting one's group identity is more important than pursuing the truth. Maintaining "our righteous ingroup against a nefarious outgroup"[4]—whether it is protecting the Second Amendment, abortion, or racial homogeneity—is seen as a source of security, strength, and superiority.

WHAT CAN WE DO?

We need to own up to our responsibility for what we do to create the disruption, disharmony, and disconnections in the world. We need to be clear about whom we are supporting to overcome our collective shadow and whom we are not. Are we supporting cultures and religions that are focused on material gains that could destroy the planet? Or are we supporting cultures and religions that are deeply connected to the earth to provide a stable and secure base for development of "a global tribe, *unus mundus*, a seamless thread of humanity woven into the earth's elements and emerging from those same elements."[5]

Our first response to our collective shadow should be to listen and see what is already happening to reduce its power. There are movements for racial justice, for protection of the environment, and for social equity to which we can add our voice and financial support.

A major stumbling block for white people who read this book is likely the shadow of systematic racism. For example, I had this dream:

> A young Black man is supposed to be working on a group project. I suspect he is pursuing his own agenda and not the group project. I later discover he had written out his plans and had given them to me. He was not holding anything back. He had a lot of energy.[6]

3. Jung, *On the Psychology of the Unconscious*, 1917.

4. Fisher, "Belonging is Stronger than Facts."

5. Delio, *Re-Enchanting the Earth*, 89.

6. When people of color appear in the dreams of whites, it is one more indication of how whites embody racism. It is important to notice all of the ways we are involved in racialization. Then it may be possible to transform and take responsibility for our level of awareness and consciousness.

I believe the dream is about trusting that BIPOC have given us all the evidence we need to commit our energy to support necessary change, as in my dream. We know what to do; it is time to do it. As my own shadow is being integrated into my awareness, the shadows of others are also being stirred by our existential crises. Besides looking inwards, we are responsible for taking action that is needed to cede and disperse the power we hold unfairly.

In another dream I saw that people were gradually being turned into compliant beings, which led to their destruction. But a group emerged that realized what was happening and took over after they realized that this destruction had happened in other cities.

My reflection on the dream was that the key was awareness: becoming conscious of what is happening in the society, finding others who are resistant to the collective shadow of illusion and deceit, and are willing to take action.

As more of us connect to Universal Consciousness and develop greater wholeness, a new collective consciousness will evolve. We know from quantum biology that we are quantumly entangled. The field of our individual consciousness is connected with the consciousness of another person or people.[7]

We contribute to this connectedness and wholeness when we bring out the goodness in the people with whom we are entangled, which is everyone. Our emotional attachments lead to action-oriented empathy. When we genuinely see the other person, we are able to meet them where they are. We can develop deep empathy if we look to communities that have developed empathy by engaging in a mutual learning process. The dominant culture needs to listen to and learn from other cultures.

The "hundredth monkey" story is true.[8] When a critical mass of enlightened beings emerges, our present will be transformed into a world without war, poverty, tribalism, fear, deprivation, and violence.

---

7. Trinka and Lorencová, *Quantum Anthropology*, 83.

8. The story is that unidentified scientists were conducting a study of macaque monkeys on the island of Kōjima in 1952. These scientists observed that some of the monkeys learned to wash sweet potatoes, and gradually this new behavior spread through the younger generation of monkeys through observation and repetition. The researchers observed that once a critical number of monkeys was reached (i.e., the hundredth monkey), this previously learned behavior instantly spread across the water to monkeys on nearby islands. https://www.mazzastick.com/change-your-thoughts-to-change-your-life/

This may seem like a dream. It is. But our dreams and intuitions can awaken us to the reality that it is not the Earth that is in danger. We are the ones in danger, the species that is destroying the biosphere. It is us, the Homo sapiens, who have lost touch with Consciousness in the Anthropocene we have created. Herrmann states:

> Many religious figures in history have become momentarily at-one with the Cosmos. But the door to the universe's deeper or higher recesses is in us all. We may all step through it, for brief moments, and when we do, we are open to oneness or unity of being ... What we need, according to Jung, are dreams and intuitions that can provide more objective facts.[9]

Think about the values supported by the social media you visit and the TV channels you watch. Are they consistent with your values? How does your relationship to technology affect your interaction with others? The Internet is the global consciousness. Since each of our actions changes how Google works, we have an obligation to only retweet and "like" posts that add positive value to the global consciousness, not destructive values. Put out fires, don't stoke them.

We are all interconnected spiritually through Universal Consciousness. As we develop our larger Self, we have the potential to connect with all minds within the same field of infinite Consciousness. The fuel of that spirituality is unconditional love and compassion for others and for self. The more we can experience and express that love, the more healing and Wholeness we will see.

With a unitive consciousness of Wholeness, we can approach each other with openness, curiosity, and respect in the quest for common ground that will substantially dissolve the polarizations. We can heal ourselves and the collective shadow that is destroying our world. We can move from our addiction to material greed and power to the all-infusing compassion of Universal Consciousness.

CAN TECHNOLOGY HELP?

Technology can play a critical role in global Consciousness, but it depends on how artificial intelligence (A.I.) is developed. A.I. can widen the gaps between rich and poor. Ilia Delio says, "The electronically connected

9. Herrmann, *William James and C.G. Jung*, 381.

post-human can play a critical role in the world's future, if post-human life is guided by the religious dimension of inner conscious life."[10]

Just as medieval Christians believed in both a physical space described by science (natural philosophy) and a nonphysical space that existed outside the material domain (heaven), the advent of cyberspace returns us to a realm that operates on a different plane of the material world. Cyberspace offers a new transcendent space of possibilities that facilitates a connection to Consciousness.[11]

In cyberspace, we can explore personal identity and develop friends around the planet as we gather in shared thoughts and ideas. During the COVID-19 pandemic, the Internet pushed us toward a new planetary community, sharing our fears and hopes online in Zoom conferences, joining in a common concern for our future.[12]

The consciousness of the creators of our technology, particularly A.I., must be raised. There are many issues of equality. How will power be distributed in the new evolving systems—to whom or to what? Efforts to develop global guidelines for the ethical use of artificial intelligence will be futile if they fail to account for the cultural and regional contexts in which A.I. operates. Without more geographic representation, a global vision for A.I. ethics will only reflect the perspectives of people in a few regions of the world, particularly North America and northwestern Europe.[13]

> We must start to prioritize voices from low – and middle-income countries (especially those in the Global South) and those from historically marginalized communities. Making responsible A.I. the norm, rather than the exception, is impossible without the voices of people who don't already hold power and influence.[14] We also need to value all forms of consciousness. Our typical human-centric view of life does not value the intelligence of animals like octopi, who have consciousness distributed in all eight of its arms. We must realize our limitations, remain curious, and embrace the possibilities of consciousness that is present everywhere.[15]

10. Delio, *Re-Enchanting the Earth*, 184.

11. Delio, *Birth of a Dancing Star*; Delio, *Making All Things New*; Delio, *A Hunger for Wholeness*; Harari, *Homo Deus*; Harari, *21 Lessons for the 21st Century*; Olson, "Is Technology Creating the Future?" in *And God Created Wholeness*, 193–194.

12. Delio, "Internet Easter," blog, April 6, 2020.

13. Gupta & Heath, "A.I. Ethics Groups."

14. Gupta & Heath, "A.I. Ethics Groups."

15. See Coleman, *A Human Algorithm*.

Reader Reflection: How can you contribute to reducing the power of our collective shadow?

If you are highly motivated to be a person who contributes to transforming the Anthropocene with Consciousness, the next chapter, *Chapter 10: Becoming an Agent of Holism,* is for you.

Chapter 10

BECOMING AN AGENT OF HOLISM

"For there is always light if only we're brave enough to be it."

—AMANDA GORMAN, "THE HILL WE CLIMB," JANUARY 20, 2021

Reader Reflection: At this point, how brave are you to be the light to transform the Anthropocene with consciousness of Wholeness?

NEW DAY WITH NEW POSSIBILITIES

DURING THE SIXTIES AND SEVENTIES, I was aware of the New Age consciousness, the hippies, and the interest in spiritualism. I regularly went to the Esalen Institute (California) for workshops by psychological and spiritual leaders. Eastern spirituality that came to the West at that time (even affecting the Beatles) introduced us to these ideas.

But the current hunger for Consciousness is different. This is a different time and a different me. It is serious now. The future of our species and our biosphere is at stake. In the old model of enlightenment, the individual transformed but the world stayed the same. In the new model, the world can be transformed through the individual. We can consciously evolve together.[1]

---

1. The concept of the old versus new model is from Cohen, *The Evolution of Enlightenment*.

I now have a strong sense of the infinite, the oneness and wholeness of the universe that buoys me as I face our existential crises. I sense that I am an agent of wholeness, at once mystical and prophetic.

I feel mystical about the unity and sacredness of my reality and prophetic as I see the need to speak out about racial, economic, environmental, and social inequalities. Jan Phillips has poetically captured the difference between mystical and prophetic:

> A mystic draws attention to the unity and sacredness of what is, while a prophet is one who speaks out when the unity is disrupted. Like yin and yang, they are two aspects of one whole—the inner and the outer, the stillness and the action, the silence, and the song. [2]

This chapter is a call to join the ranks of mystics and prophets to transform the Anthropocene with consciousness of Wholeness.

CALL TO HOLISM

Becoming an agent of holism[3] requires a jolt in our Surface and Liminal consciousness. It requires a change of heart, a reinvention of ourselves. Like the shamans of the indigenous peoples, agents of holism can pull deep energy from Consciousness and be a source of spiritual energy for themselves and others.

Being an agent of holism requires a radical surrender of self to Consciousness. In this surrender, we each must follow our own unique path to find out who we really are and what we are being called to do by the universe.

If we care about fostering a nurturing Earth for all its creatures, including us humans, we need to ask: What shall I do now? How will I extend the generative forces of the world? How can I be an instrument of progress?

2. Phillips, *No Ordinary Time*.

3. The author of the concept of holism, derived from the Greek root holos (whole), was the international statesman, Jan Smuts. His book *Holism and Evolution*, published in 1926, had a significant impact on thinkers like Albert Einstein. He desired to write a sequel, *Spiritual Holism*. Sadly, international affairs, and particularly his support of Winston Churchill and the Allied effort during World War II, precluded him from achieving that dream. According to Smuts, our view of reality, and hence the quality of our engagement with life, would be incomplete without a fundamentally transformed view of spirituality capable of transcending dualism. Thanks to Claudius van Wyk for this information. For more information, see https://holos-earth.org.

The answer to these questions is: Choose opportunities that are strongly associated with your feelings of joy, peace, love, and faith. Avoid choices that lead to feelings of agitation, fear, confusion, and depression. St. Ignatius trusted that "there is a vital spirit, an absolute, that draws us, yet lies hidden. If we are to see its features, answer its call, and understand its meaning, we must plunge boldly into the vast current of things and see whether its flow is carrying us."[4]

Beyond our Surface and Liminal consciousness of ideas, thoughts, images, and feelings, we need to discover who the "I" really is in Bedrock consciousness. Who are we at the deepest level—behind our thoughts and feelings or others' thoughts and feelings about us?[5]

An introverted agent of holism has an inner realization of peace, the oneness of all reality. An extraverted agent often experiences the wonder, bliss, and rapport with nature and all of creation.[6] Because they are energized by people, extraverts light a fire under a group's energy and fan it, drawing out the introverts. Both introverts and extraverts can express their reality for the benefit of others.

Teilhard de Chardin's wartime letters to his cousin Marguerite Teillard-Chambon are remarkable for a man working as a stretcher-bearer, living for the most part in the mud of the trenches, and at the same time taking advantage of his rest periods to jot down on paper his notes and plans.[7] The following excerpt from *Writing in Time of War* captures the zeal and zest of someone who takes on the challenge of being a mystic and an agent of holism:

> Anyone who has the mystic's insight and who loves will feel within Something that seizes him and drives him on to absolute integrity and the use of all his powers. He is willing to self-correct and self-develop in order to become resonant to the pulsations of the rhythm of reality; the mystic makes himself docile to the unobtrusive demands of grace. To increase his creative energy, he tirelessly develops his thought, dilates his heart, and intensifies his activity. He labors unceasingly to purify his affections and to remove all blocks to the light.[8]

4. Teilhard de Chardin, *Writing in Time of War*, 27–28.
5. Rohr, *What the Mystics Know*.
6. Kourie, "Weaving Colorful Threads," 5.
7. Teilhard de Chardin, *Writings in Time of War*, 134.
8. Teilhard de Chardin, *Writings in Time of War*, 134.

Teilhard asks a would-be agent of holism to plan, open the heart, and *"just do it,"* as the Nike slogan commands.

WHAT IS A MYSTIC?

The traditional image of a mystic is of a person who contemplates fantastical things and withdraws from the world. A more appropriate image is a person who looks at the smaller picture with a perspective of the big picture—with love. They see the reality of all three dimensions of Consciousness.

Mystics are free from the three powers that typically hold humans in bondage: ego, possession, and violence. They are not co-opted by a need for security, possessions, or the illusion of power. A true mystic is connected to all other humans and to all of creation.[9] Soelle says:

> Genuine mystics, like Buddhist bodhisattvas, don't renounce the world for the sake of a private spiritual illumination. Rather, they use the enlightenment they've achieved to do something about the world's ills.[10]

Mystics have a strong tolerance for uncertainty and ambiguity, and see things from a transcendent perspective—a capacity to suppress their linear rational and logical abilities and see the infinite and wholeness beyond material reality. Mystics are open to receive the grace that arrives from Consciousness, without falling into the magical-thinking trap that sees all outcomes as either good or bad.

Mystics are able to lose the illusions of their Surface consciousness and reduce their defensiveness. They pay attention to their shadow. They detach from cultural distractions and delusions of TV and Internet culture. I am still working on this.

Mystics are needed to support politicians and other leaders who have the moral imagination to strive for inclusion of diverse voices, leaders who will hold the values of compassion and empathy for our future, leaders who are pursuing Wholeness.

9. Soelle, *The Silent Cry,* 293.

10. Soelle, *The Silent Cry,* 293.

ARE YOU ALREADY A MYSTIC?

Mystics[11] are leery of strict doctrines, principles, and spiritual hierarchies imposed by religious institutions, even to the point of rebelling and developing their own rules. They value their personal experience with the divine. They use their intuition to pursue answers to such existential questions as, "Why am I here?"[12]

They do appreciate spiritual practices that provide new perspectives, trigger insights, and support personal growth so they can be helpful to others. They are comfortable with uncertainty but generally feel there is a purpose and all-encompassing love in the Universe.[13]

DEVELOPING NEW SKILLS

Long before we were conscious thinking beings, our cells were reading data from the environment and working together to mold us into robust, self-sustaining agents. We think with our whole body, not just with the brain. We draw on experiences and expectations to predict likely outcomes from a relatively small number of observed samples. When we approach a new problem, most of the hard work has already been done. Our body and brain, from the cellular level upwards, have already built a model of the world that we can apply almost instantly to a wide array of challenges.[14]

As we become more aware of Consciousness and our true Self, we become a new type of person. We develop a deep relationality and entangled life with the consciousness of others. Our relationships become more complex and creative (me *and* you = us). The "I" is a dynamic, ongoing construction of relationships formed by the constant flow of shared information.

Increased access to Consciousness is not dependent on a solitary person going on a vision quest or the like. It now becomes a shared venture into a unitary world.

We will develop a new generation of improved transformational practices that will enable many more of us to draw more efficiently and

11. Cara Hebert, a writer about transformative spirituality, describes 10 characteristics of mystics that will help you answer that question. Hebert, "Am I a Mystic?"

12. Hebert, "Am I a Mystic?"

13. Hebert, "Am I a Mystic?"

14. Medlock, "The Body is the Missing Link."

systematically upon normally inaccessible resources of imagination, creativity, and spirituality.[15] We will pass our higher level of consciousness onward to the next generation of hominids.

A major challenge for those who wish to communicate their holistic perspective is starting a conversation with a person who holds a different view of reality. Approaching people with different worldviews requires affection and respect. Begin by slowing down to create a space to listen attentively and ask open-ended questions that invite exploration of topics of mutual experience and importance. Engage with a sense of wonder and awe rather than judging what side they are on. Search for areas of common enjoyment and agreement.

Learning how they experienced and reacted to events in their life will help both you and the other person gain a wider perspective. Recounting an event that was difficult to live through may transform the event to something satisfying to remember.

David Brooks says, "In the Talmudic tradition when two people disagree about something, it's because there is some deeper philosophical or moral disagreement undergirding it."[16] Mutually digging down to the underlying disagreement and then to the underlying moral disagreement below it can resolve the conflict.

Be patient, pause to create an opening for other connections. Acknowledge what the other is saying, and take time to let the relationship develop. Joining a coffee group at a local diner or attending a discussion in the other person's church are good places to start the conversation.

DEVELOPING A CRITICAL MASS

Is it possible that a critical mass of people will access Consciousness and develop a mystical, unitary worldview of Wholeness before it is too late for our life on this planet? Will there be an awakening, a cultural revitalization where entire groups will shift their perceptions regarding fundamental questions of self, citizenship, justice, and transcendent reality? Will there be a realignment and restructuring of our institutions, and redefinition of our social goals? Have our old systems and culture broken down enough for something new to emerge? Diana Butler Bass says:

---

15. Kelly and Kelly, *Irreducible Mind.*

16. Brooks, "Nine Nonobvious Ways to Have Deeper Conversations."

> To proclaim an American awakening is underway is to claim
> . . . that we are in an extraordinary period of change, one brought
> about by lost faith, social disorientation, and cultural distortion,
> that will result in bringing in those who have been marginal-
> ized *and* create a politics whereby more can flourish. To insist that
> this is an awakening is to insist on hope—that distress and chaos
> are not the last word.[17]

Bass hopes that we will not return to an illusory past. This could be a time when leaders will emerge to shift humanity to a new level of consciousness, to reach a higher moral ground, a fundamental and distinctive moral elevation, that supports us in shedding our fears and giving hope to each other as we take progressive action.

I am a member of the *Holos Project* based in Spain that is building alliances and networks around the world for agents of wholeness and organizations as it supports a global shift to a holistic perspective. The project hopes to provide a transformative perceptual lens to influencers, leaders, and policymakers. The intention is to redirect human endeavor in a way that applies human resources and ingenuity to sustainable natural resource management. This is aimed at ultimately actualizing a deeper human potential.[18]

The Project has developed a core group who will curate the initiative, leading to a second, broader invitation to all those who will participate in researching the specific theory, philosophy, and science of holism as an alternative epistemology for this time. The hope is that this will lead to the application of holism as a perspective and approach in all domains. Ultimately a network, an alliance of holistic practitioners, will be created for mutual support and enrichment through the sharing of knowledge and experience, and the shared generation of opportunities.

The critical mass of agents of holism will be those individuals who harness their inner capacities through transformative practices and cultivate the resilience needed to navigate the challenges of Surface consciousness and still be compassionate and empathic.

To see what consciousness is telling us, we need to slow down and see what is trying to break through.

17. Bass, "Awakening Now?"
18. The Holos Project, https://holos-earth.org.

Reader Reflection: How much time and energy are you prepared to commit to be an agent of holism for your friends and associates? What will be your contribution?

What is the way forward? Our major institutions will need to confront their own shadows and develop a consciousness of Wholeness. Is that possible? We explore that in *Part IV: Transforming Our Institutions.*

Part III Implications

RESPONDING TO THE CRISES

ANDREW HARVEY SAYS THAT WE have attracted these crises to us: climate change, pandemics, species extinction, and capitalism ("an orgy of greed"). But he believes these crises could potentially birth a new embodied divine humanity—a new human. If we radically surrender in love to Consciousness, the grace of divine intelligence will transfigure humanity. Our dark night can be healed if we are willing.[1]

The dark night of our individual and collective souls can be healed if we face our shadows and realize that is not who we are. If we are humble, recognize the pain, and do the inner work, we can reach out to others as agents of holism and find our true Selves. When we put our egos aside, a loving community will emerge. The mystics have already developed the path through the obstacles and out of the global dark night. Will we choose to follow it?

MOVING TOWARD OMEGA

When we access Consciousness, we move toward greater Wholeness. As we become more whole, we do not become perfect. We remain the differentiated people that we are, but the various aspects of our fragmented selves develop a harmonious relationship. We sense the energy of the larger interconnected Whole. We know we belong to specific people, place, and

---

1. Harvey and Baker, *Radical Regeneration*.

community. We know that what we already have is enough and that all we need is to use it wisely.[2]

Teilhard's scientific studies and his faith brought him to the conclusion that human consciousness would continue to complexify and move toward a Center of universal convergence, which he called the Omega Point. He believed that we are becoming grouped together, connected to one another, because we are being pulled forward by the Center up ahead.[3] He wrote:

> When I consider the inexorable nature of the universal impulse, which for more than 600 million years has ceaselessly promoted the global rise of consciousness on the earth's surface, driving on through an endlessly multiplying network of opposing hazards, I am forced to the conclusion that the Earth is more likely to stop turning than is Mankind, as a whole, to stop organizing and unifying itself.[4]

For Teilhard, the end of time is a maturing rather than a destruction.[5] As the cosmos is becoming progressively more conscious or spiritualized, matter will shift to spirit as humanity self-develops and becomes one with the divine.[6] Death will simply be another phase of growth. We will merge with Consciousness in a union greater than ourselves.

Just as the Sun broadcasts fusion energy to the Earth, Consciousness is pushing humanity to a realization of who we truly are by fusing those things that keep us separate to make wholeness. An agent of holism is like the Sun, putting forth wholesome energy and a new story. We matter more than we think.[7]

These are the challenging questions as we move to *Part IV: Transforming Our Institutions*. What have I done as an agent of holism? Have I meditated on our common humanity? Have I reached out to the most marginalized? Have I moved toward a greater love, complexity, and relationship with the Earth? What have I done to move humanity toward Omega?

---

2. Adapted from Benner, "Perfection and the Harmonics of Wholeness," 62–63.

3. Teilhard de Chardin, *The Divine Milieu*, 45, 47.

4. Teilhard de Chardin, *The Future of Man*, 152.

5. Thanks to Dr. Anita Wood for these quotes from Teilhard. She has created a "Center to Center" process for people to develop consciousness with other people, using the content and evolutionary principles of Teilhard.

6. Teilhard de Chardin, *The Divine Milieu*, 122.

7. Thanks to Rhett Gayle for the Sun metaphor.

Part IV

TRANSFORMING
OUR INSTITUTIONS

INTRODUCTION:
MAKING TANGIBLE PROGRESS POSSIBLE

WHY HAVE OUR INSTITUTIONS FAILED to prevent our human-made existential crises? It is because of dualism—the separation of Consciousness, the essence of reality, from matter, its physical manifestations. Humans at the pinnacle of material creation can do whatever they want.

Human institutions are massively entangled with all biological systems of the planet. As controllers of the Anthropocene, whatever we do affects our relationships with animals, plants, the air we breathe, and the food we consume.

If it is imperative that individuals be agents of holism, how much more important is it for institutions to use their resources and power to foster the welfare of the biosphere and its inhabitants, including us? We are all responsible for our crises because of our entanglement, but, as we explore in these chapters, it is ultimately our institutions that need to be held accountable. What is possible?

The sad truth is that our institutions are not just "too big to fail," but even too big to be criticized or changed. They are good and necessary, in and of themselves, but they have become idolatrous. "They are sanctified, romanticized, and idealized necessities that are saluted, glorified, and celebrated in big paychecks, golden parachutes, parades, songs, rewards for loyalty, flags, marches, medals, and monuments. There is an underlying, unspoken social agreement that certain evils are necessary for the common good."[1]

From my experience as a consultant, substantial change in institutions and organizations requires a transformation in consciousness—a change of mind and heart in a leadership that embodies and leads the change. Leaders who have integrated their shadow can create the conditions that allow institutions to change.

To transform the Anthropocene, we need the tangible progress that only institutions can provide. Only institutions can create the conditions necessary for the full development—physical and spiritual—in individuals. Organizations do this by creating healthy workplaces, enabling the arts to flourish, promoting scientific research, educating about wholeness, and creating inclusive technology.

Feeling guilty is not enough. Mistakes in the past can move us forward if we commit to immediate changes. This is how institutions deliberately develop their consciousness.

There are signs of hope as seen in the inter-faith and inter-spiritual movements, the greening of many corporations, and the extension of educational and mental health opportunities. To evolve to the next stage of consciousness, our institutions and organizations must go to the edge of Consciousness where creativity happens and where evolution can take new leaps.[2] What Matthew Fox said is required for greater personal wholeness is also required for institutional transformation:

> The future requires all of us to dive deep and return, surfacing with the wisdom, the mysteries, and the truths we learned from diving . . . [to] birth a new culture in business and economics, in politics and religion, in art and engineering, in community and agriculture, in the media and law—one that . . . makes it easier to be sustainable and to survive as a species.[3]

In the next three chapters, we will explore this "deep dive" described by Fox and explore how our institutions and organizations can include enchantment and creativity as a first step to meet our long-term needs as conscious beings, rather than meeting the immediate needs of the economic and political system.[4]

1. Adapted from Rohr, *What Do We Do with Evil?*, 79–81, 83, 85.

2. Fox, *Meister Eckhart*, 274.

3. Fox, *Meister Eckhart*, 275.

4. Harari, *21 Lessons for the 21st Century*.

PART IV: TRANSFORMING OUR INSTITUTIONS

An authentic connection with Consciousness will transform our institutions to provide progressive political and economic action, social justice, compassion, and a global ethic.

Chapter 11

REFRAMING RELIGION

Reader Reflection: Can religious institutions be an effective catalyst for transforming the Anthropocene? How?

THE RELIGIOUS IMPULSE

DURING THE EARLY EVOLUTION OF the human species, there was no separation between the identity of a person and the Oneness of creation. Everything was a part of the whole. The whole experienced and expressed itself through embodiment in living species. As our human species became self-conscious and more conscious of the mysterious world around them, they imagined there was a divine presence that is separate from us.

The separation increased as humans named and represented the fundamental forces in their environment in paintings on cave walls, clay tablets, parchments, and Scriptures. They named and described these forces in ways that controlled their actions, sometimes to good effect (morals, goodness, justice) and sometimes with bad effects (war, prejudice, etc.). As an impulse to awaken and implore the divine presence they named and described, religions were developed.

Teilhard said religion is a function of consciousness—that which gives form to the free energy of the earth.[1] He said, "To my mind, the religious phenomenon, taken as a whole, is simply the reaction of the

---

1. Delio, *The Hours of the Universe*, 15

universe as such, of collective consciousness and human action in process of development."[2]

The spiritual and the material were ontologically the same, but the human need to create concepts and terms to describe the ineffable—that which is too great to be expressed in words—created a metaphysical gulf between the human and their sense of a divine presence.[3] Because we continue to create new religious concepts and terms, awareness of the paradigm of Consciousness needs to be an essential component of that religious thinking and language, otherwise the labels we put on ourselves and our religious institutions mask the truth that we are a part of a greater Whole.

RELIGIOUS INSTITUTIONS

For many, especially older Americans, religious institutions are an essential part of their identity. Their religion provides a place and purpose to gather for the many things it offers: social community, companionships, and opportunities for spiritual growth. However, in America, new surveys show membership in communities of worship has declined sharply in recent years, with less than 50 percent of the country belonging to a church, synagogue, or mosque.[4]

For those who do not hold a traditional view of God, when participating in a church service, almost everything that is said, read, sung, or performed must be reinterpreted. Rather than jettison the archaic language found in the Sunday service, good churchgoers feel bound to "be nice" and "not rock the boat."[5]

The problem is that institutional religion remains tied to a static past, rejecting evolution as the operative narrative of biological life, and espousing religious beliefs based on ancient metaphysical principles.[6] Delio asks:

> Do we want to maintain our old religious doctrines, practices, rituals, and beliefs even though these cater to our individual needs?
> . . . Our present systems were built on the needs of the individual,

2. Teilhard de Chardin, "How I Believe," 118.

3. Lawson, "Complete in Manhood."

4. Walsh, *America is Losing Its Religion.*

5. This quote is taken from a response by Vosper to a question from *Progressive Christianity.* The Rev. Gretta Vosper is a United Church of Canada minister who is an atheist. Her best-selling book *is With or Without God.*

6. Ilia Delio, blog, June 28, 2020.

but they are battling against the forces of change. One of the greatest forces of resistance today is religion.[7]

Churches of the future that want to be part of the healing of the nation and the earth will need to overcome their spiritual myopia (short-sightedness) that fosters our cultural wars and update their scientific, sociological, and cosmological understanding to tell a bigger story, one that "includes and validates wisdom from all religions and spiritual traditions."[8]

Houses of worship could be places for dialogue in small groups where the expression of Consciousness is not limited or stilted by a narrow theology and worldview. Healthy religions help people live the ultimate questions of life and strengthen authentic faith experiences. Ideally, religions promote a sense of awe and reverence, encourage thoughtful reflection and questioning of any kind, and build bridges among people.

As church members access all dimensions of Consciousness and develop greater wholeness, their spiritual core will shine and be visible to others. Together, church members will unite to let go of practices that are no longer life-affirming. "Church" can then become unique, inspiring, and welcoming of all.

WHAT ABOUT THE "NONES"?

Many of those who have left institutional religion ("nones") are longing for a believable faith, a theology that integrates religion and science, the sacred and the secular.

A survey by the Pew Research Center in 2018 found that people who have left the church still have a religious or spiritual attitude, although they do not believe in God.[9] Many are suspicious of any religion, ideology, or worldview that claims infallibility. Yuval Harari put it this way:

> As we come to make the most important decisions in the history of life, I personally would trust more in those who admit ignorance than those who claim infallibility. If you want your religion, ideology, worldview to lead the world, my first question to you is: 'What was the biggest mistake your religion, ideology, or worldview

---

7. Ilia Delio, blog, March 2020.
8. Johnston, *Overcoming Spiritual Myopia*.
9. Samuel, "Atheists Are Sometimes More Religious than Christians."

committed?' 'What did it do wrong?' If you cannot come up with something serious, I for one would not trust you.[10]

Across the United States, small groups of adult seekers are on a spiritual journey to construct a believable and science-compatible theology. For them, God is much more a verb than a noun, which is consistent with science's understanding that the universe is primarily processes, happenings, and events, not fixed matter. For most, this quest still assumes the existence of a God, albeit a liberal, enlightened God. I have been a member of such groups in Minnesota, Florida, and Tennessee.

To contribute to substantial change in the Anthropocene, institutional religion must let go of doctrines and practices that are not life-affirming in order to embrace the new possibilities in the paradigm of Consciousness.

CONSCIOUSNESS AND GOD

In traditional Christian theology, "God" is seen as an abiding presence, an endless mystery, *the great more* of the universe. Religion based on the concept of God can be comforting, healing, and reassuring, and represents our highest values. But for many religions, what "God" decides is the judgment of a human person.

Use of the word "God" often comes with assumptions and experiences. When the word "God" is spoken, it usually evokes a sense of power and control. The hope is that God will respond to a petitionary prayer.

When the word "Consciousness" is spoken, it evokes attention and listening. Consciousness is a resource of wisdom and love we tap into to help us evolve. God is top-down direction and creation. Consciousness is bottom-up, a more inclusive sense of a Presence greater than me. Consciousness is the ground that underlies all religions, spirituality, and science.

For people who connect to both the mystery and the personal qualities of what is ultimate, the word "Consciousness" may feel cold. For others, Consciousness is the underlying energy field and unifying force drawing us into a hopeful future.[11] If we think of Consciousness as a resource, our partner as we evolved, we get away from thinking of the Presence of the divine as omni-powerful. Consciousness gives us hope that there was

---

10. Yuval Noah Harari, 21 *Lessons for the 21st Century*, 220.

11. Gober, *An End to Upside Down Thinking*, 218.

intelligence from the beginning and that there is an unfolding—the Universe is going somewhere.

Mark Gober, a major proponent of Consciousness as fundamental, prefers the term "One Mind" instead of "God." Jesus' quote "I and the father are one" is translated by Gober as "Jesus, as an individual whirlpool, is one with the stream." He translates the quote "The kingdom of God is within you" as, "Even though you are an individual whirlpool, you are composed of the same water that makes up the full stream of reality." Gober believes "words such as *father* and *God* have become so culturally off-putting that we can overlook what is actually being said."[12]

Reimagining our use of God-language should reduce the belief that there is a force in the universe that intervenes or dictates codes of thought or behavior. Progressive Christianity and atheism have not significantly dislodged the belief in a Being that fundamentalists keep evoking. Some preachers of traditional Judeo-Christian morality are so identified with goodness in the official values of the traditions that they are completely unconscious of their own shadow.[13] How else can we account for pastors inviting un-masked crowds into a confined indoor space during the COVID-19 pandemic because "God would protect them"? Talk about magical thinking!!

Many contemporary theologians have stopped using the word "god" but have not seen Consciousness as fundamental.[14] Even in her exercise of 101 ways to say "god" in her book, *With or Without God*, Greta Vosper, an ordained minister of the United Church of Canada and a self-professed atheist, did not list the word "consciousness."[15] Whatever we call the divine, it is not an "it." Thoughts, forms, subjects, and objects arise out of human consciousness. The essence of formless existence can't be described. We can only point to it.

---

12. Gober, *An End to Upside Down Living*, 51.

13. Gober, *An End to Upside Down Living*, 146.

14. Robinson, *Honest to God*; Beitman, *Connecting with Coincidence*; Taylor, *After God*; Kearny, *Anatheism*; Kellerer, *Cloud of the Impossible*; Todd, *The Individuation of God*.

15. Vosper, *With or Without God*, 236.

CONSCIOUSNESS AND JESUS

In the last 2,000 years or so, people evolved who had extraordinary abilities to understand and experience Consciousness. The universal truths that are at the root of all major world religions can be known directly when in a state of consciousness which, although rare, has been achieved by individuals in all cultures as far back as it is possible to ascertain. Whether through a gift of nature or through rigorous training, Jesus and others have received special states of consciousness; and their insights form a common core to all religions.[16]

Jesus was so fully in communication with Consciousness as an indwelling presence that he exemplified that wisdom and love in his actions and sayings. He could see beneath the surface of the natural order and imagine a more whole, more loving, and more peaceful way of being in this world.

For example, Jesus related this parable in the Gospel of Thomas (109):

> The kingdom is like a person who has a hidden treasure in his field, (of which) he knows nothing. And [after] he had died, he left it to his [son]. (But) the son did not know (about it either). He took over that field (and) sold [it]. And the one who had bought it came, and while he was ploughing [he found] the treasure.

Like the father and the son, many are unaware of what is in the fields of consciousness. People living in Surface consciousness need to go to Bedrock consciousness, to their treasure, Universal Consciousness. The new owner in the parable finds the treasure when he plows the field. We also must dig beneath the Surface to find Consciousness. We have to disturb what is superficial to discover what is deep.

Jesus taught others to awaken their imagination to the same possibilities. He challenged the people of his day, and our day, to free themselves from the narrow religious, social, and political attitudes that kept their minds shallow and their souls small.[17]

Cynthia Bourgeault is a modern-day mystic, Episcopal priest, writer, and internationally known retreat leader. She says that Jesus' vision of a whole and unified human being is typical of the Perennial Wisdom that there is a "larger, non-dual mind" that is the "seed of personal

---

16. Goff, *Galileo's Error*, 205–206.

17. Wright, *Reimagining God and Religion*, 127.

consciousness."[18] Deepak Chopra also describes Jesus' non-dual reference to the location of God as both inner and outer at the same time, where the dividing line between reality "in here" and "out there" "softens, blurs, and ultimately disappears [as] reality shifts from dualism to unity."[19]

Jesus regularly initiated a connection to Consciousness. His disciples sensed this ability to transcend the normal plane of existence and access the inner depth of Consciousness. He set aside his personal ego and power needs for the sake of others and for the sake of the invisible source he called Abba.[20] His presence is still "so commanding and whole that he abides in lives in the psychic realm, ever ready to speak to the inner self within each of us."[21] "Christ" is the name that points to the wedding of human and divine consciousness. Being attentive to "Christ Consciousness" is to become more conscious, whole, and attentive to our True Selves.

CONSCIOUSNESS AND THE HOLY SPIRIT

What has been characterized as Spirit is the presence of Consciousness in the beauty, truth, and goodness pervading our world. Physical science restricts itself to providing information about the behavior of particles, fields, and space/time but tells us nothing about their intrinsic natures. The equations of physics allow us to predict the behavior of matter with great precision. But it is the intrinsic nature of matter, its inherent consciousness, that breathes fire into those equations.[22]

The light of Consciousness is a useful metaphor for the Spirit. It is the force and energy that enhances life and wholeness. It works in us to bring us to who we truly are.

Practices of Kabbalah, Christian mysticism, Sufi meditation, Buddhist meditation, and devotional prayer, among others, are ways people have accessed this larger sense of consciousness and connection with the world just beyond their sight.[23]

---

18. Bourgeault, *The Wisdom Jesus*, 62.

19. Chopra, *The Third Jesus*, 87.

20. Chopra, *The Third Jesus*, 87.

21. Murray, *The Bible Beyond Religion: Witness to the Evolution of Consciousness*, 187.

22. Goff, *Galileo's Error*, 129.

23. Goff, *Galileo's Error*, 23.

IMPACT OF CONSCIOUSNESS

In 2010, Philip Clayton, a distinguished philosophical theologian who teaches at the Claremont School of Theology, wrote *Transforming Christian Theology for Church and Society*.[24] A few years later, I led an adult study group in Florida, following Clayton's guidance to develop our own Christian theology. We engaged "the concrete and practical concerns of both church and society." We wanted to make progressive Christianity so attractive that "evangelicals, charismatics, mainliners, and Roman Catholics would joyfully discuss it over a meal together."[25]

Now, I would argue that the new paradigm of Consciousness can inform a different transformation of Christianity more aligned with Gnosticism, Christian mysticism, and Christ Consciousness.[26] We need to ask new theological questions: If Consciousness is the unifying experiential field at the ground of all reality, is God within consciousness? Is Consciousness within and an expression of God? Has Consciousness been what people have always intuitively sensed, and have been referring to as "God" all along?

A comment from a reader of a draft of this book, a retired Methodist pastor, describes the kind of impact the new paradigm of Consciousness can have in revisioning Christian scripture:

> In my morning meditation I was reading Acts 2:42–47 about the experience of the new community after Pentecost. Verse 42 jumped out at me: *A sense of awe came over everyone.* In the context of how this sense of awe affected their changed behaviors described in the rest of this passage, my mind went to what I had been reading in your writing about Consciousness. Surely, they were connected to each other through this Consciousness! And this is what Jesus was teaching them. You are helping me to see scripture in a new light.

The Abrahamic religions are based on the mystical experience of their founders: Moses and the burning bush, St. Paul's Damascus Road vision, the revelation of Allah dictated to Muhammad by the archangel Gabriel, and the pillar of light that fell on Joseph Smith. The lives of these men were turned around by the numinous experience. All were changed by the

---

24. Clayton, *Transforming Christian Theology*.
25. From the endorsement on the back cover of Clayton's book by Brian D McLaren.
26. Rohr, *The Universal Christ*.

explosive force when their consciousness connected to the reality at the heart of all reality—Consciousness.

People today are searching for something to believe in, a power that vitalizes and dynamizes life. To move society to greater wholeness, we must not be afraid; we must dare to dream to work for the good of the whole. If the Consciousness paradigm can re-envision the worldview of Christianity and other religions in the world, we will chip away at the tribalism, fear, and violence we see in cultures that are rooted in theism.

Consciousness can provide the long-awaited interbeing framework that transforms static religious structures from their tribal, dogmatic, creedal, and institutional fetters toward a viable spirituality of the future—a formless, science-based spirituality without walls that at long last has universal, inter-spiritual application.

We have lost touch with the moving flow of spirit. The Taoists, Buddhists, and Christian mystics have been trying to tell us that for many years, but we haven't been able to develop a framework in the secular world that makes sense. There is an appropriate role for philosophical and scientific descriptions, but those descriptions need to lead us to a deeper experience of Consciousness, the spiritual energy wave that pervades the Universe.

The critical test for any religion is: "Does it make space for otherness? Does it acknowledge the dignity of difference?"[27]

Matthew Fox, after exploring eighteen myths and teachings that all religions share, offers an analogy for inter-spirituality: "one river, many wells." He quotes Meister Eckhart as saying divinity is a "great underground river that no one can dam up and no one can stop." I believe that Consciousness is the underground river of shared wisdom that all religions hold in common. Matthew Fox puts it this way:

> The way I picture it, each religion has its own well that draws from this common river, so we need to honor different wells, then journey deep into whatever well we choose till we come to the one river, the source that is beyond all names. As Nicholas of Cusa says: 'Even though you are designated in terms of different religions, yet you presuppose in all this diversity one religion which you call wisdom.' [28]

Religion can be a positive "river" in dismantling structures of patriarchy and oppression, recognizing the emergence of gender and racial

27. Sacks, *The Dignity of Difference*, 61.

28. Fox, *Meister Eckhart*, 276.

plurality, and empowering local communities to structure their own religious identities.[29]

Religion needs to be a vital part of the new Cosmic story. Religion matters. Religion is the mystical dimension of life that gives us the truths that makes life worth living, like loyalty, love, joy, delight, eros, virtue, kindness, and creativity. These truths are portals to Consciousness and meaning. Religions do have an enormous shadow but so do governments and all other cultural, social, and political institutions. Religions have expressed the consciousness of their time and culture.

At the core of the great religious traditions is a realization that we are one with Consciousness. The rituals of religion are the unique self of that religion—the unique quality of meaning, intimate communion, and relationship of the infinite and the finite. There are underlying principles of religions that are universal. But a religion is much more than that.

The new story about religion's contribution will not emerge from a reduction to the universals but from their intimate, culturally untranslatable, ecstatically urgent hope to merge with the divine.

> *Reader Reflection: Do you think religious institutions can play a significant role in reducing our collective shadow? What changes will need to be made?*
>
> Going Forward: Imagine your own religious or spiritual faith as a river or well that leads you to the One river of the wisdom of Universal Consciousness.

29. Ilia Delio, blog, October 2020.

Chapter 12

REIMAGINING EDUCATION AND WELL-BEING

OUR ECHO CHAMBER

THE LAST EVOLUTIONARY JUMP THREE hundred millennia ago gave us larger and more complex brains than we needed for our immediate survival. As we evolved, we developed an ability to create and manipulate symbols to give us greater control of the three-dimensional world.

As we have settled into our identity in our Surface consciousness, many have become locked "inside an echo chamber of like-minded friends and self-confirming news feeds, where their beliefs are constantly reinforced and seldom challenged."[1] The fear of change and desire for order and stability keep many from thinking for themselves. This is the power of "groupthink" that is impervious to more and better information and facts.

The echo chamber has been accelerated by the Internet, social media, talk shows, the pandemic and electoral politics. As many were isolated and impoverished by the pandemic, they turned to polarizing radio and TV talk shows to make sense of their predicament. Both the left and the right were in their own echo chambers and less likely to engage respectfully with "them." There was less learning, less diversity, less engagement, less nuances. The several years leading up to the 2020 presidential election provided fertile ground for conspiracy theories.

---

1. Harari, 21 *Lessons for the 21st Century*, 225.

During the pandemic, many became sick, lost loved ones, lost jobs, endured long periods of isolation, or witnessed terrible suffering while serving on the front lines. Some reached a breaking point of grief, anxiety, despair, and anger that opened them to believe in a Big Lie and conspiracy that led to the January 6 attack on the Capitol.

The keel of a sailboat keeps the sailboat upright. Education is the keel of our culture. It needs to be more about values and fostering the mental health of the children. Hitler was abused by his alcoholic father and neglected by his depressed grief-stricken mother. This does not excuse Hitler's evil. However, Hitler is an extreme example of an antisocial leader being abused as a child. Research indicates that 0.1 percent of all humans are born with a tendency to be truly antisocial which is cultivated from early childhood. That means that in a population of over 300 million in the United States, we have more than 300,000 people to worry about.

WHAT KIND OF EDUCATION AND MENTAL HEALTH SUPPORT IS NEEDED?

We can't teach education in the Western culture without bringing in the body and spirit, without nurturing the souls of our children. The Center for Compassion and Altruism Research Education emphasizes starting with self-compassion, self-acceptance, and self-kindness, which are different values than self-absorption, self-esteem, self-indulgence, and narcissism.

True education and psychological help are NOT just more information. A lot of the anguish and grief we feel about the plight of our civilization and the planet is Consciousness speaking. The power and guidance beyond our own egos is awakening us to our resistance to change.

Basic science, technology, engineering, math (STEM), liberal arts, and counseling programs are necessary, but our next evolutionary jump needs to be to Consciousness, which is beyond the reach of the active mind. There we can confront our personal and collective shadows.

Rather than listen to the voices of fear, criticism, and cruelty that shape the way we see, how we feel, and what we do,[2] we need to pay attention to what comes up in our dreams and meditations. Opening our hearts to support innovative educational and mental health systems will likely be the result. Good health and well-being are essential for being whole. What makes

2. Rohr, "Order, Disorder, Reorder," blog, August 25, 2020.

your heart sing and ignites your passion about life is influenced by the level of consciousness in your family, close friends, and larger community.

We need to create learning contexts for holistic practices of acceptance, compassion, and empathy at all levels of education and mental health. In doing so, we must seek solutions that benefit the whole system and unify that which separates us. Consciousness flows through every level of human consciousness, but our Bedrock consciousness must be trained and cultivated to provide the wisdom and love needed in our Surface consciousness to function in the world. This will take time and patience. It is dependent on the individual's readiness and desire to find their true Self.

Moving toward Wholeness is the next step toward transforming the global culture.

VALUING INTUITION IN EDUCATION

In *Finding Reality: Four Ways of Knowing*, I argued that to be fully aware of the reality and meaning of any life situation and to fully develop our identity, we need to use four ways of knowing:

1. Accessing the wisdom of others (Authority),

2. Finding hard evidence (Empiricism),

3. Valuing our own intuitions (Insight), and

4. Relying on our own experience (Praxis).[3]

Any of these four ways of knowing can be a portal to Consciousness, but it is #3, our *intuition,* that lets us see beyond the occurrences in Surface consciousness and enter Bedrock consciousness to access Universal Consciousness. Our visions, insights, thoughts, ideas, dreams, epiphanies, and hunches seemingly come from nowhere. Whether produced internally through meditation or brought to our awareness from outside sources—although provisional and fleeting—intuitions are valuable guidance from Consciousness.

Meister Eckhart calls intuition the "spark of the soul," a doorway into the kingdom of God, meaning the place where justice and compassion flow. Both Eckhart and Einstein would agree that our culture lacks intuition. For those who trust in the essential goodness of people, returning intuition to the center of education would be a truly transformative event.

3. Olson, *Finding Reality.*

A truly deep education would develop a person's spiritual intelligence and encourage intuition and trust in one's own authority. Accepting the reality of a mystical experience develops wisdom and creativity as the person moves through the dimensions of Consciousness and levels of awareness of reality.

The important questions are: What are we educating for? What values do we want to communicate? Who is profiting from education as it is executed today? Are people happy educating and being educated? Is the whole person being valued, including their mental state? Where is the joy?

THE INCLUSIVE VALUES OF EDUCATION

Besides developing our intuitive capacity, deep education is about discerning and imparting life-affirming values.

The current values of American education are derived from the Industrial Revolution. Schools are modeled on the factory, shuffling each student to disconnected subjects. The emphasis on getting a job devalues the arts, music, and dance—aspects that fulfill us as humans. Fox explains:

> The object was for them to get enough information to pass the test, to be a finished, marketable product . . . that is, to return to the factory. An alternative value and wisdom-based education that honors creativity and imagination, nature, intellect, the body, the soul, and practice can renew our feelings for who we humans really are and for reconnecting with the universe—inwardly as well as outwardly.[4]

For the vast majority in our society, what new values they will accept remains unseen. The polarizing U.S. election in 2020 made clear that the two identity tribes in the United States do not accept many of the values of the other tribe. The few who try to remain neutral in the middle are pulled by the strong magnets of ideologies of the left and the right.

Similarly, wresting our future from the grip of fossil fuels seems impossible—our addiction is too strong, affordable options are too few, and the powers that defend the status quo are mighty. We cannot be freed by chipping away at this millstone. We must begin to live into new values by becoming partners with Consciousness and acting in unfamiliar, untested

---

4. Adapted from Fox, *Meister Eckhart*, 261–263.

ways: resilience, collaboration, wisdom, balance, moderation, vision, accountability, and self-giving love.[5]

LEARNING FROM THE "OTHER"

Science has verified the ancient spiritual truth that we are all part of one another. When we meet the "other," we can state as "a moral declaration and a spiritual, cosmological, and biological fact: You are a part of me I do not yet know."[6]

Education that promotes inclusion creates something new out of each interaction. My colleague Glenda Eoyang says, "teach and learn in every interaction." We won't ignore the majority of the people in the world who are different from ourselves. We will be reaching out and asking people who have different opinions to join with us.

How do we create trust and authentic relationships? How do we inspire hope and honor? How do we validate the Other? How do they know that we really see who they are?

Ubuntu is an African concept we can use to form an "Us" consciousness. The core of Ubuntu is that a person is a person through other people. We affirm our humanity by recognizing the Other in his or her uniqueness and difference. In a sense, we create each other. As a political philosophy, Ubuntu encourages community equality and the distribution of wealth. Ubuntu implies that everyone has different skills and strengths we need to be complete.

The Consciousness that looks through your eyes is the same as the Consciousness that looks through my eyes. When we have an authentic conversation, forgive each other, and hold the gaze between each other, we can create "Us" now. There is only one of us here. Consciousness is the great includer!

With an elevated consciousness we do not have to be so cautious in our initiatives and responses. We can take risks to "step on eggshells." Differences that have been formidable in the past can be worked through. The need for minority communities to filter responses in order to make the majority comfortable will be reduced.

In this new community of consciousness, change will start within us and grow incrementally from where we are.

5. Adapted from Rohr, "Order, Disorder, Reorder," blog, August 26, 2020.

6. Kaur, *See No Stranger*, 10–11.

SEEING WHOLENESS

Deep education is holistic. It combines intellectual values, intuition, and feeling. A values-based and wisdom-based education is the synthesis of body and mind, of wonder and curiosity. As Einstein said, "There is no true science which is not emanated from the mysterious. Every time a person must be filled with wonder and awe just by looking up at the stars."[7] The universe tells us that everything is enfolded into everything.[8]

David Bohm described the universe as a whole or implicate order that is "our primary reality . . . the subtle and universal reservoir of all life, the wellspring of all possibility, and the source of all meaning."[9]

The seemingly random events in daily life are interpreted as random because of our limited perspective. If we could see through a wholeness lens, the randomness would disappear.[10] When we are in an intuitive, Liminal state, our brain's filter unlocks to reveal our connections to everything.

Recent research has found that a belief in wholeness and oneness is related to a more inclusive identity that reflects concern and compassion for the welfare of other people, a sense of connection with nonhuman animals and aspects of nature, and a recognition of our common humanity, problems, and imperfections.[11]

What would happen if all political parties recognized and believed in oneness even as they are asserting their values and political beliefs?

HEALING THE PSYCHE

The global COVID-19 pandemic is an example of an immense, collective liminal space where there are many uncertainties and limited controls. The vulnerability and openness of liminal space allows room for something genuinely new to happen. As individuals quarantined, they also had the possibility of creating a new understanding of essential existential questions: who am I, what is life, and what is my purpose?

We must make room for psyche's role in our recovery from ego intoxication—that we know it all, can have it all, can change without changing

7. Kaur, *See No Stranger*, 280.

8. Bohm, *Wholeness and the Implicate Order*, 225.

9. Ó Murchú, *Quantum Theology*, 62.

10. Gober, *An End to Upside Down Living*, 60.

11. Kaufman, "What Would Happen If Everyone Truly Believed Everything Is One?"

and, above all, that we know how to fix it. Parts of that recovery will come in new forms, some of which we may be inclined to dismiss because of the flood of information and misinformation or irrelevant distractions.[12] Harari reminds us:

> People need the ability to make sense of information, to tell the difference between what is important and what is unimportant, and above all to combine many bits of information into a broad picture of the world.[13]

To stay relevant—not just economically but socially—we will need a lot of mental flexibility and great reserves of emotional balance to constantly learn and reinvent ourselves. We will have to repeatedly let go of some of what we know best and learn to feel at home with the unknown and what emerges from Consciousness.[14]

> The decisions we make in the next few decades will shape the future of life itself, and we can make these decisions based only on our present worldview. If this generation lacks a comprehensive view of the cosmos, the future of life will be decided at random.[15]

The educational strategies to implement a Consciousness paradigm will recognize inherent connectivity of life and the self-organizing capacity of nature to synchronize its many parts into larger wholes. Paradoxically, the innate connectivity does not suffocate individual expression but liberates it into deeper forms.[16]

When we open to the collective field of consciousness, the boundaries of the individual ego dissolve, but as the ego is diminished, a "deeper form of individuality is being birthed . . . one that thrives in this subtle give and take, an individuality with expanded responsibilities and a longer time horizon."[17]

We live in a world that we may experience as being full of contradictions, false alternatives, zero-sum games, paradoxes, and unresolvable evils. It is foundationally unjust, yet we must work for justice in order to find our own freedom and create it for others. By giving ourselves to this primary

---

12. Bernstein, *Living in the Borderland.*

13. Harari, *21 Lessons for the 21st Century,* 128.

14 Harari, *21 Lessons for the 21st Century,* 270–71.

15. Harari, *21 Lessons for the 21st Century,* 267.

16. Bache, "Teaching in the New Paradigm," 2016.

17. Bache, "Teaching in the New Paradigm," 2016.

human absurdity, which shows itself in patience, love, and forgiveness toward all things, we recognize that we are all complicit in this mixed moral universe. This gives us the active compassion we need to work for social change.

> *Reader Reflection: What do you think of this proposed massive leap in educating for greater consciousness and restoring our nation's mental health? Is it impossible? What would make it possible?* [18]

Perhaps business and government can help. We explore that in *Chapter 13: Reforming Business and Government.*

---

18. Adapted from Rohr, *What Do We Do with Evil?*, 79–81, 83, 85.

Chapter 13

REFORMING BUSINESS AND GOVERNMENT

IN THE PREVIOUS CHAPTERS, I have argued that Consciousness is moving us collectively to action on behalf of nature and civilization and, thus, on behalf of our own survival.

But how many of our organizations are willing to support individuals who have insights from Consciousness to birth a new social-economic-political structure? How many will join the struggle to create a just holistic and unfragmented community?[1]

Is a values-first economy possible? Justin Rosenstein and his colleagues in the One Project Team believe that "the power of modern information technology combined with age-old wisdom about cooperative use of common resources can create . . . new systems that optimize for the will and well-being of the people and the planet."[2] The team imagines an accessible, user-friendly website and mobile app, built as a commons-based, open-source platform cooperative, that allows any community to govern itself through collective intelligence, productive deliberation, and intelligent resource distribution. As an example of what can be done, they cite how in 2020, Taiwan gracefully managed its COVID-19 outbreak through digital democracy tools that built trust and leveraged citizen participation.

We can no longer give special credence to the current dominant story about why things are the way they appear to be. Do we have the courage to work through the ongoing healing of our wounds? Do we and our

---

1. Adapted from Holmes, *Race and the Cosmos*, 194–195, 196.
2. Rosenstein, "The Architecture of Abundance," 35–36.

organizations have the bandwidth to actualize the vision of Rosenstein and his team?

> *Reader Reflection: As you reflect on your connection to business organizations and/or government agencies (as manager, employee, owner, or customer), can they be moved to a higher level of consciousness? How?*

CONNECTEDNESS

With a connection to Consciousness, we can begin to view daily business situations not just as paths toward financial security, but as opportunities to embody and practice interconnectedness. Gradually we begin to view colleagues, customers, and even competitors as less separate from us. For example, in Zoom meetings and conference calls, we might begin to speak with more consideration for others or adjust the tone in our emails.

Our business objectives might even shift. While still concerned about making a profit, we realize that creating win-win outcomes for all parties is conducive to our own success. Business becomes a vehicle through which we can become more aligned with Consciousness.

During the COVID-19 pandemic, our connectedness has become obvious. What one person does, such as not wearing a face mask, can have tragic consequences for hundreds of other people. Not behaving wisely, as if you are immune from the consequences that bind other human beings, is an existential selfishness.[3] When we insist on our "rights," we are "stepping on the very fabric of what makes our life worth living."[4]

The new connectedness and concern for the whole begins deep within us. We will also develop new economic structures when we practice having "enough," when we put aside shallow wants and demands, and support communities—not merely to gather and keep for ourselves, but to support others in those communities.[5] Matthew Fox calls this "deep economics":

> Deep economics is less about earning money than it is about fostering and preserving our lives and the common good.[6]

3. Myers, *Saving God from Religion.*
4. Dewey, *The Fourth R*, 2.
5. Fox, *Meister Eckhart*, 279–280.
6. Fox, *Meister Eckhart*, 280.

PURSUIT OF PROFIT WITH CONSCIOUSNESS

Americans are losing trust in leaders and the information emanating from every sector of our society. Ironically, outside of the voices in their echo chambers, the CEOs of business institutions are currently the most trusted to tell the truth and fix problems.[7] The problem is, if the CEOs are pursuing profit as an end in itself, the leader is blind to societal values and is deaf to any message from Consciousness. Anita Roddick, an environmental and business activist, asks: Is it possible to move business from private greed to the public good? If demanded by organization leaders and the consumers themselves, business can be responsible incubators of the human spirit, rather than only produce more material goods and services.[8]

Accessing Consciousness improves a CEO's ability to recognize the truth that underlies the illusion of our system of profit. Jeffrey Eisen says, "The problem is not that corporations operate for a profit; it is that the present economic system, not reality, defines this profit. The corporation makes the profit, not humanity and the global ecology."[9] Eisen goes on to describe the result:

> At this time in history, a corporation can destroy an ecosystem, pollute a river, and impoverish an indigenous culture, but if it makes a monetary profit, if it costs less to destroy part of the world than the earnings such destruction engenders, the corporation is deemed profitable—and the investors realize a comfortable return on their investments . . . That is not a profitable corporation but a subsidized one, one that, in whole systems terms, operates at a substantial loss. By whom is it subsidized? By the countries that house it, by the ecosystem of the globe, by you and me, and by every person that walks or will walk the earth.[10]

Eisen believes that a realistic approach to build corporate accountability and responsibility starts with redefining profitability itself—making it profitable for the corporation to contribute to the human sphere and unprofitable for it to consume without at least recycling and restoring. This will require making corporations accountable for their real costs of doing

7. *21st Annual Edelman Trust Barometer*.

8. Fox, *Meister Eckhart*, 247.

9. Eisen, *The Omnius Manifesto*.

10. Eisen, *The Omnius Manifesto*.

business. To reach this level of awareness, CEOs will need to regularly access Consciousness.

We need an economic system that works for not only humans, but water and soil, forest and air, everything that lives, and the generations to come.

WHAT ABOUT THE PUBLIC SECTOR?

Appealing as are Roddick's views about the responsibility of business, are they realistic? For years there has been a general agreement between government policy-makers and corporate executives that a corporation needs to maximize profit so the economy would grow to the benefit of everyone. The government's role was to facilitate that goal while imposing necessary regulations for public health and safety.

Despite a paralyzed government in 2020, Binyamin Appelbaum, an economics professor, holds out the hope that it is government, not corporations, that will create the incentives for "good behavior and laws."[11]

Applebaum believes that government has the most powerful means to foster the public interest and still support economic growth by investing in education, infrastructure, and research.[12] The role of government is to ensure that those profits do not come at the expense of society.

But again, adopting Applebaum's hope ignores the reality of its limitations. After all, our government reflects our divisiveness and polarization. Jamelle Bouie points to the essential issue—our illusion that we will solve the worst aspects of our political culture, a potent brew of destruction, lawlessness, and authoritarianism, with our current level of consciousness.[13]

The pandemic has taught that we need to pay attention to who we put in political office. Can we build a new political system on what the wreckage of the pandemic has forced us to see?[14]

David Brooks put it this way: "We have to dispense with the fantasy that after the next miracle election our side will suddenly get everything it wants. We have to live with one another."[15]

---

11. Appelbaum, "Blaming Milton Friedman," A:22.

12 Appelbaum, "Blaming Milton Friedman," A:22.

13. Bouie, "Our Illusions," SR:11.

14. Pollan, "In Search of a Politics of Resilience: On the Field and in the Mind."

15. David Brooks, "What the Voters Are Trying to Tell Us," 19.

THE POWER TRAP

Whether it is business or government, the biggest obstacle to a higher collective consciousness is the desire for power and control for the benefit of the few. A lust for power keeps the focus on Surface consciousness where reality is defined in strictly material and cultural terms. Everything is viewed through those two lenses.

Even the most benevolent institutions co-opt new members into the power trap almost unconsciously. David Brooks phrased it this way:

> They send ambitious young people powerful signals about what level of dissent will be tolerated while embracing dissident values as a form of marketing. By taking what was dangerous and aestheticizing it, they turn it into a product or a brand. Pretty soon key concepts like 'privilege' are reduced to empty catchphrases floating everywhere.[16]

Yuval Harari says that great power acts like a black hole that warps the very space around it. The closer you get to it, the more twisted everything becomes. People who have power like CEOs, political leaders, or government executives receive deference from all who hope to gain from the use of that power.

Leaders who want to escape the black hole of power that is based on existing knowledge and conventional wisdom need to access their intuition and Consciousness.[17]

Organizational leaders need to think of power as a coat they put on when they need to but have enough respect for the coat to take it off. For example, Dwight Eisenhower exercised power as a general and president, but had the humility and wisdom to warn us about the power of the military-industrial complex.

Leaders who access Consciousness experience a "oneness" with everything, a unity consciousness. John Renesch says this about leaders informed by Consciousness:

> They regularly transition from being a victim and dodging personal responsibility and believing that one's circumstances are someone else's fault. They give up control and surrender to something greater than oneself. This goes beyond feeling simply connected, since connected can still imply separateness, not unity.

16. David Brooks, "This is How Wokeness Ends," A22.

17. Harari, 21 *Lessons for the 21st Century*, 228.

Experiencing unity one no longer experiences reality as a duality—either/or, right/wrong, questions/answers. Pure knowingness, freedom, and peace prevail in this non-dual realm. While there may be preferences, there are no attachments. Leaders in this state share leadership and are self-directed and have fewer moods or obsessive thinking states. As a result, there is reduced stress and more openness to change for the leader as well as others in the organization.[18]

ORGANIZATION CHANGE

For 30 years I have been an organization development (OD) consultant. That means I was the catalyst for changing an organization's culture or mission to be in greater alignment with human values of fairness, equity, and empowerment. I have worked with managers and employees of business, non-profit, and government organizations by gathering both objective and subjective information about how well the organization was functioning—its culture, climate, and ethics. When the data points were presented to organizational leaders, change would happen in ways that moved the organization forward.

I principally worked in the Surface and Liminal domain. Occasionally a manager would reach Bedrock consciousness and act on information from Consciousness. For example, this happened when my NTL Institute colleagues and I began a diversity program in a federal government agency. The human resource executive called us into his office. He told us that after waking up in a sweat after a dream in which he was punishing Blacks in the agency, he initiated the diversity program. It was a clear example of the deep stirring at the Bedrock that can bring about dramatic personal transformation, and, in this instance, transformation in a workplace.[19]

CHANNELING THE ENERGY OF CONSCIOUSNESS

While writing this book, I had this dream:

> A leader in a scientific/technical organization is excited about what my team can bring in partnership with his organization. It was a

18. Renesch, "Conscious Leadership Coaching."
19. Olson, *And God Created Wholeness*, 142.

high-tech company that needed the human dimension, although I observed that many were highly functional. I tell a person that this is about the human aspects of the organization. My team has not put together a coordinated approach. I ask each of the other three team members to give a short speech. They are reluctant. The leader has brought together the whole company in a row. I light up each section of the company. In the first phase, one member goes into a refrigerator to give his speech. He emphasizes Mark Gober's theory of consciousness. I tell him I had planned to include that in my speech.

The dream reflected my own nervousness and uncertainty about containing and channeling my energy and knowledge of Consciousness. In the dream, I was upset about the bursts of information from my impulsive side. I felt that the person in the refrigerator was uncontrollable, like quantum energy. I needed to caution and cool this impulse in a refrigerator. I even had to close the door.

I believe the dream was a warning that implementing change in our institutions will be fraught with exciting possibilities for collaboration, but that as the transformative power of Consciousness is gathering, we need to exercise some caution, some boundaries, and some channeling of the energy. Claudius van Wyk suggests these actions until a "new ethos is able to take hold":

> We need clear behavioral norms and regulations to ensure economic activity benefits society whilst critically also sustaining living systems. So, we can identify three dominant forces: the *market*, the *state*, and *civil society*. Certain more genuinely progressive countries are already attempting to encourage a continuing dialogue between representatives of those three forces, to identify those economic norms, to inform their laws, and to enable economic activity that is life-enhancing rather than extractive.[20]

Frederic Laloux and Ken Wilber, authorities on consciousness in organizations, say that the level of consciousness in an organization cannot exceed the level of consciousness of the leader.[21] I would also add that the level of consciousness of any shared leadership group is a cap on what is possible for the organization. If you have a leadership position at any level, think of the implications of these observations.

---

20. Claudius van Wyk, blog, October 13, 2020.
21. Laloux and Wilber, *Reinventing Organizations.*

Reader reflection: After reading this chapter, do you feel more or less optimistic about moving your organizations to higher levels of consciousness? What action steps can you take?

Part IV Implications

A RADICAL SOLUTION

OUR CURRENT PARADIGM OF REDUCTIVE materialism has polarized us—left and right, citizen and noncitizen, white and nonwhite, the poor and the affluent, science believers and climate change deniers.

The COVID-19 pandemic has also revealed other chasms. Why is the economy so fragile for some? Why is it that white Americans have a "propensity to dispense with Black life . . . a pathology that authorizes public murder for the sake of white supremacy?"[1]

Socrates observed more than 2,000 years ago that sometimes the best we can do is to acknowledge our own individual ignorance. The greatest crimes in modern history resulted not just from hatred and greed, but even more so from ignorance and indifference.[2] How can anyone understand the web of relations among thousands of intersecting groups and organizations across the world?[3] How can we act morally when we have no way of knowing all the relevant facts? Harari explains:

> The world has simply become too complicated for our hunter-gatherer brains. Most of the injustices in the contemporary world result from large-scale structural biases rather than from individual prejudices, and our hunter-gatherer brains did not evolve to detect structural biases.[4]

1. Lebron, "White America Wants Me to Conform."
2. Harari, 21 *Lessons for the 21st Century*, 233.
3. Harari, 21 *Lessons for the 21st Century*, 235.
4. Harari, 21 *Lessons for the 21st Century*, 234.

We now have a world of structural biases with algorithms that maximize profits. The human spirt has been diminished. Rohr says the great chain of being has been broken. We are separated, looking for control. We need a compelling story to tie everything together. Our current stories are based on the belief that reality is material and physical. Without a spiritual binding, that belief is too shallow. The narrative needs to be deeper to unite us.

When Abraham Lincoln referred to "the better angels of our nature," he was talking about Consciousness. He said this in the middle of the Civil War. Can we find our better angels today? There are examples of institutions and companies putting people and the planet ahead of profit. This is an incremental change of the traditional triple bottom line of profit, people, planet. In the Bible, people interpreted dreams that led to radical change. This is the kind of change we need.

The most common feature in NDE experiences is the feeling of being surrounded by and submerged in absolute Love, an overwhelming, indescribable Love—another name for Consciousness.

In the new story I discuss in *Concluding Thoughts: A Compelling Story*, we are all interconnected spiritually through Universal Consciousness. As we develop our larger Self, we have the potential to connect with all minds within the same field of infinite Consciousness. The fuel of that spirituality is unconditional love for self and others. The more we can experience and express that love, the more healing and Wholeness we will see.[5]

The new faith in Consciousness will allow us to approach each other with openness, curiosity, and respect in the quest for common ground.[6] Individually and collectively moving through the dimensions of Consciousness will substantially dissolve the polarizations. As Delio states:

> The key to our future lies in relational wholeness. Only together can we co-create a new America where there will be neither black nor white, slave or free, male or female, but all will be one in a new power of love, a nation empowered from within by a new religious consciousness, oriented toward the flourishing of life.[7]

Unitive consciousness can heal ourselves and the collective shadow that is destroying our world. We can move from our addiction to greed and power to the all-infusing love and unity of Universal Consciousness.

5. Adapted from Alexander and Newell, *Living in a Mindful Universe*, 103.

6. See Schneider, "Today's Biggest Threat."

7. Ilia Delio, blog on racism, June 28, 2020.

Concluding Thoughts

A COMPELLING STORY

OUR CURRENT SITUATION

TOBY ORD, A PHILOSOPHER WHO studies our species' existential risk, says that a social, economic, and environmental train wreck is just around the corner, as is a dramatic unraveling of the human and planetary systems. He places the risk of our extinction during the twenty-first century at one in six—the odds of an unlucky shot in Russian roulette. Besides asteroids, super-volcanic eruptions, and stellar explosions, there are the threats we have created for ourselves: nuclear war, climate change, pandemics, and other novel methods of man-made destruction still to come, such as empowered artificial intelligence unaligned with human values and engineered pandemics.[1]

A reminder that we are living in the Anthropocene and controlling evolution came in the Spring of 2021. The much-anticipated arrival of the cicadas after 17 years underground did not happen in many places because they had been covered with concrete.

On top of these realities, the United States is witnessing a political and social realignment unfold in real time. In 2020, collective fear and concern about the pace of change and instability drove our politics. Even after inauguration day, the disinformation that drove that fear continued—and continues today.

1. Ord, *The Precipice*.

140

We have recently split into several Americas, all with distinct politics, social networks, and media channels. Jim VandeHei, founder of Axios news network, says:

> Now, more than ever, is the time to read and reflect: Our nation is rethinking politics, free speech, the definition of truth, and the price of lies. This moment—and our decisions—will be studied by our kids' grandkids.[2]

Unfettered capitalism has directed the flow of resources toward those who hold power and away from those who produce goods or provide services.

Many people are being radicalized and increasingly attracted to violent movements. Far-right groups are recruiting and developing their cultural, intellectual, and financial capacities in a variety of mainstream settings, including college campuses, mixed martial arts gyms, clothing stores, online gaming chat rooms, and YouTube cooking channels.[3] Miller-Idriss demonstrates how young people on the margins of our communities are targeted in these settings, and how the path to radicalization is a nuanced process of moving in and out of far-right scenes throughout adolescence and adulthood.[4]

Currently we are living a collective dream—a rational, analytic, ego-driven dream. Many of our spiritual stories have not been consistent with science and have lost their appeal. Our material and secular culture has highjacked spirituality and left a void that we try to satisfy materially.

TRANSFORMATION OF THE HUMAN HEART

To deal with our current crises, we need to enlarge our hearts. If we only suppress our personal and collective shadows without a radical collective change to our hearts and lives, it is only a matter of time before another, even more aggressive virus, environmental catastrophe, and/or social revolution emerges. If we do not deal with the shadows, they will just be repressed again until another spark relights the fire. When we access Consciousness, we see our cosmic significance and the ego loses its freedom to

---

2. VandeHei, "Our New Reality."

3. Miller-Idriss, *Hate in the Homeland.*

4. Miller-Idriss, *Hate in the Homeland.*

act merely in its own self-interest. Our outer development must be matched with inner development. Kornfield notes:

> In Zen they say there are only two things. You sit. You tend the garden. You quiet your mind and open your heart. And then, with natural care, you get up and tend the garden of the world.[5]

Consciousness will be able to transform the Anthropocene if we participate. When a critical mass of people has adopted or adapted the paradigm of Consciousness to their own belief system, there will be a shared experience of enlightened awareness beyond the personal ego.[6] We will recover a shared moral code "that cooperating, promoting the common good, is the right thing to do."[7]

With the light of Consciousness, religious, educational, business, and government institutions will inform the revolution the world needs—a global transformation of the human heart.

CONSCIOUSNESS AS SOURCE

Consciousness continually interacts with sentient beings at a Bedrock dimension of consciousness. Our three-dimensional worlds of phenomenal reality are constructed by the brain together with Consciousness. This theory unifies intelligence (Mind), the physical world (Matter), and the generative process of self-creating.[8]

When the filters of the brain, heart, gut, and sensory organs are opened, Consciousness also informs our Liminal and Surface consciousness. We have a free will to try to avoid Consciousness, but also, we have the ability to listen, to learn, and to assent to what we are being called to be and do.

This theory of creation is consistent with both mysticism and theism, including the "process theology" worldview that a divine presence interacted with the creative field and the natural laws of the universe by offering possibilities, rather than forcing anything to happen.

---

5. Kornfield, "Open Hearts, Open Minds," 208.

6. Inspired by Cohen, "The Evolution of Enlightenment."

7. Curry, Mullins, and Whitehouse. "Is It Good to Cooperate?"

8. The theory is neither a monism nor dualism. Perhaps it can best be labeled as a dual aspect monism, a fundamental duality at the heart of reality that is neither mind nor matter – a weird middle ground. Thanks to Finley Lawson for this comment.

The theory is also consistent with Max Velmans' account of Reflexive Monism. If Consciousness is the source of everything, it integrates realism and idealism, dualism and monism, ordinary experience and mystical experience, the mind and the brain.[9]

For mystics, the hard problem of Consciousness is, "How can something physical emerge from mind?" For the materialist, the hard problem is, "How can consciousness emerge from physical structures?" A quantum perspective provides a synthesis of both worldviews: What we observe as distinct and separate in our Surface consciousness of space and time is not separate at the deeper quantum level. The reality we experience through our senses emerges from a deeper underlying quantum reality.

THE NEW STORY

We live in the grip of a deeply flawed story under the spell of materialism. The paradigm of Consciousness provides the foundation for an authentic new narrative, one informed by Perennial wisdom—the patterns that are always true, beyond anecdote and cultural history—that holds everything together in sacred meaning.[10]

The new story also needs to include the wisdom of our great religious traditions and the forward-leaning edge of science. The spell of materialism needs to be broken by the wisdom of Consciousness that integrates the material and spiritual, science and faith. As Delio puts it:

> The mysterious new universe calls for a renewed sense of divine mystery in the cosmos, a new religious myth, a new narrative that draws us . . . into these cosmic waves that are, in some fundamental way, the source of our lives.[11]

To learn and embrace this new story, we need to empty ourselves, like the professor in the following story:

> Nan-in, a Japanese Zen master received a university professor who came to learn about Zen. Nan-in poured a full cup of tea for his visitor and kept pouring.

9. Velmans, "Reflexive Monism."

10. The definition of Perennial Wisdom is adapted from Rohr, *Things Hidden,* 22, 24; and *The Wisdom Pattern,* 112–113.

11. Delio, *Hours of the Universe,* 5–6.

The professor watched the overflow until he could no longer re-
strain himself. 'It is overfull. No more will go in!' 'Like this cup,'
Nan-in said, 'you are full of your opinions and speculations. How
can I show you Zen unless you first empty your cup?'[12]

Reality is not dependent upon whether we understand it or not. There
is reality that is novel and creative beyond our immediate understanding.
We discover it as we develop our human consciousness. We are agents of
our own deep insights into that reality. A compelling vision of Wholeness
will emerge when a critical mass of humanity has direct experience with
Consciousness.

Ervin Laszlo, a renowned systems scientist, sees hope in a rising collective evolution in consciousness. For centuries, the old paradigm has
divided consciousness from matter, the soul from the body, nation from
nation, and science from religion, creating a world of divisions and wars.
But awareness of ancient truths is emerging in connections and collabora-
tions in pockets all around the world, inspiring a feeling of empathy and
compassion, of belongingness and, ultimately, of love.[13]

David Korten is hopeful that a viable human future will be guided
by a more complex and nuanced view of the world based on twenty-first-
century economics. These new economic lenses recognize that a nation's
gross domestic product tells us nothing about whether growth and financial exchange are beneficial or harmful to people and the planet. He says:

> . . . Life's wellbeing depends on resilient communities that control
> their resources to meet essential daily needs; and that the only
> legitimate purpose of any human institution—including those of
> business and government—is to serve the well-being of people
> and Earth. To meet this requirement, markets need rules created
> and enforced by democratically accountable governments.[14]

A deep connection to Consciousness can sustain the patterns of liberal
democracies like ours, which many in the world still look to as a model. The
collective wisdom of Consciousness opens our eyes to our systemic social
injustices and enables us to make decisions and take actions that move us
toward the ideals of Life, Liberty, and the pursuit of Happiness.

---

12. Reps and Senzaki, *Zen Flesh, Zen Bones: A Collection of Zen and Pre-Zen Writings*,
5.

13. Laszlo, *What is Reality?*, 272.

14. Korten. "Telling a New Story," 266.

Everyone must realize their hidden potential and become empowered to overcome inertia, take action, and be part of the solution. We are carriers of consciousness, the agents of holism. We can move above our self-centered, power-hungry materialism to be the conscious embodiment of an evolving universe. The universe beckons. Will we respond?

We can stretch out and mend the part of the world that is within our reach. We do not know which acts, or by whom, will cause the critical mass to tip toward a higher collective consciousness. Think of the impact of Rosa Parks sitting on a bus. From Estes, "What is needed for dramatic change is an accumulation of acts—adding, adding to, adding more, continuing."[15]

For an entire community to embrace a new paradigm, only 10 percent of the population needs to become convinced. At that tipping point, a paradigm can spread through social networks and alter behaviors on a large scale.[16]

At some point it is important to realize that we know enough, and it is time to act. Jeffrey Kripal puts it this way:

> After one has realized that consciousness is fundamental to the cosmos and not some random evolutionary accident or surface cognitive illusion, that everything is alive, that everything is connected and in effect 'one,' then what? Would the billiard-ball selves of the Newtonian world and the political systems and values built around them over the last few centuries make sense any longer? Would we live differently?[17]

We generally have a mindset of materialistic individualism. After a few weeks of being quarantined, our major concern was to get back to "normal" so we could resume our old life, consuming for our personal selves and families.

A new mindset connecting to Universal Consciousness, divested of insularity, and directed toward a global consciousness is needed now, a new vision for evolving life on this planet, where communities live in the flow of creative energies and in relation to the wider environment.

15. Estes, "Do Not Lose Heart."
16. Sreenavasan, et al., "Social Consensus."
17. Kripal, *The Flip*, 167.

Postscript

In writing this book, there were many instances in my dreams and in waking consciousness where I had soulful contacts with Consciousness. Every time I hoped for ultimate answers, I encountered obstacles to continuing a dialogue. For example, I had this dream:

> I am at Chautauqua Institution in dialogue with a man. We have deep, soulful exchanges. Our time is ending. I ask if he will be here next week. The answer was 'no.' I ask where he lives. He says, 'Northern Wisconsin.' I think it will be difficult to continue our dialogue.

Often, I would wake up and, before I could record a dream, it had disappeared. Attempts at meditation were often interrupted by the events of daily life. Basically, I quit trying to be intentional about finding ultimate truth and took what Consciousness afforded me in spite of my limitations. The result is that occasionally I receive what analysts would call a "big dream." For example, my Big Dream about Consciousness was on June 29, 2020:

> I pick up two Black men to meet with several women who are leading a project about justice. One of the men begins the project by climbing up a tall pole to take an egg from an eagle's nest. I could see the eagle setting on the nest. What ensues is conflict and unexpected actions in pursuit of the project.

My immediate reflection was that, as a white man, my work on consciousness must integrate my own shadow unconsciousness (Black men) and the powerful feminine archetype (the women leaders) to reach a deep understanding (the egg) of Consciousness (the eagle).

Let me unpack that dream a bit further. I often have dreams that include Black men. Over the years it is clear to me that they represent my shadow, aspects of myself that I have suppressed. These dreams often provide the energy and the courage to deal with what I am avoiding in my conscious life. In this dream, one of the men takes the initiative to "begin the project" by climbing up a tall pole. Climbing the pole is a symbol for reaching a higher level of consciousness—in this case, to reach an egg, a symbol of the beginning of everything, the cosmic whole.

That the egg is from an eagle is further evidence that the dream is about consciousness. In the Western culture, the eagle is often seen as a symbol of higher consciousness, the capacity to see the whole of everything. Before I begin the project, I check in with women who are concerned about justice. The women are symbolic of my inner *anima*, my feminine power that has deep insights about such virtues as justice. Think of Sophia[1] who in the Bible was present from the beginning to provide wisdom to everything that unfolds in creation.

The dream ends with a sense that conflict is inevitable but that there will be unexpected actions as we put together this new worldview that goes beyond the physical universe. We may be experiencing a quantum jump or a punctuated equilibrium in human evolution.

I have argued that Consciousness is the Source of the information, intelligence, wisdom, and love that was present from the beginning of time and space. Consciousness interacted with light, energy, and mass in self-creating the Cosmos. Many theologians and philosophers continue to wrestle with reconciling their sense of a divine presence and the apriority of Consciousness.

There will undoubtedly be many experiments in the sciences of self-creation to shed light on how our brains and bodies are related to Consciousness. They are likely to complement ongoing insights from the spiritual and religious disciplines, and the perennial wisdom of Earth-based indigenous worldviews. In these traditions dreams, visions, coincidences, and encounters with the numinous are all data. No data is excluded from validity.[2]

Bruce Greyson, the editor of the *Journal of Near-Death Studies*, has recently concluded that, although there is no scientific answers to what

---

1. Sophia appears in many passages of the Bible as the female personification of wisdom. She is celebrated in Kabbalah, a form of Jewish mysticism, as the female expression of God.

2. Sepie, "Listening to the Elders," 67.

happens after death, based on his 50 experiences with people who had near-death experiences, continued consciousness after death is the "most plausible working model."[3]

It may be that Consciousness manifests as variable speeds of vibrations in biological life.[4] Whatever the outcome of the experiments may be, they will affect not only scientific knowledge but civilization as a whole.

If we remain in the illusion that we live in the physical world that arose long before the appearance of Consciousness, our ability to influence reality will be determined by the level of development we can reach with our life sciences, technology, and communications.[5]

However, if we adopt the Consciousness paradigm, the science of self-creation and consciousness will quickly become a leading experimental science. In that case, we will begin to open up new possibilities of influencing the material world based on its underlying reality—a self-creating process of consciousness.

> *Reader Reflection: What is the story about reality that you tell yourself that can transform the Anthropocene?*

3. Bruce Greyson. *After: A Doctor Explores What Near-Death Experiences Reveal about Life and Beyond.* St. Martin's Essentials, 221.

4. Hunt, "Could Consciousness All Come Down to the Way Things Vibrate?" Hunt teaches psychology at the University of California, Santa Barbara.

5. Bondarev, *The New Science of Consciousness.*

GLOSSARY

THIS IS A LIST OF some of the concepts presented in this book. The meanings may differ, at least in part, from those used conventionally.

Active imagination. Facilitates an inward journey by a process of conscious dialogue with imaginal figures. As in meditation, the practice of active imagination is receptive to whatever emerges from Consciousness, but unlike meditation, a person engages with the image of the person or object that has emerged.

Agent of Holism. Surrenders self to Consciousness and becomes a source of spiritual energy for others.

Anthropocene. The evolutionary era when we human beings have become the most powerful force on the Earth, able to control the direction and pace of evolution.

Authority. A Way of Knowing that is expressed in the Surface dimension as conventional wisdom, ethics, and moral knowledge that relies on *external* authorities (codes, Scriptures, laws, or other people). *Internal* authority may be derived from *external* authority and/or through the other *Ways of Knowing*.

Bedrock dimension. Our quantum state of consciousness where space and time are not relevant. Our atoms and molecules, dreams, and spiritual experiences interact in Bedrock consciousness to access the energy of quantum possibilities and the wisdom of Consciousness.

BIPOC. An acronym referring to Black, Indigenous, (and) People of Color that highlights the relationship of Indigenous and Black (African-American) people to whiteness, which shapes the experiences of—and relationship to—white supremacy for all people of color within a U.S. context.

Brain filter theory. This theory says that the neocortex of the brain—the outer surface—acts as a filter, allowing into our Surface consciousness only the information from Consciousness that is necessary and useful for our survival and improvement or only what is possible for us to perceive. When the brain's filter is even moderately opened, we experience feelings of unconditional joy and profound connection with others.

Catholicity. The ever-evolving process of life that creates *coherence*. When we are linked to Consciousness, we have health and integrity. We are whole and attend to the "big picture."

Coherence. Occurs at the molecular level when atoms are doing the quantum behavior of tunneling, superposition, and entanglement—a circumstance where large numbers of particles cooperate. As an analogy, think of water molecules forming waves in the ocean.

Collective cultural human consciousness. A superpower that controls evolution on the planet. It will either create the conditions for wholeness—the flourishing of the biosphere and all creatures—or their destruction.

Collective Shadow. An invisible but very real, potent energy force made up of every individual's shadow. The collective shadow in the United States is materialism and individualism, which breeds overconsumption, valuing property over people, and valuing individual rights over the rights of the whole.

Crowell Model of Creation. Describes Consciousness as a guide, unifier, and transformer of information and energy into intelligence and matter. Consciousness provides stability in the transition between the beginnings and endings in every physical entity—from atoms to universes, from cells to ecosystems, from neurons to the totality of the networks of intelligence in all ordered existence.

Consciousness. A continuing connection of energy and matter.

Consciousness (capital C). Universal Consciousness.

Consciousness (small c). The consciousness (mind) present in all sentient beings.

Cycling. The repeating movement through the *Surface, Liminal,* and *Bedrock* dimensions of the *Wholeness Model.* Cycling creates a progression or spiral into a future of greater complexity. Cycling is necessary to adapt our worldviews and interpretations of events to current realities. Cycling through the levels of Consciousness prompts us to confront our shadows and develop greater Wholeness.

Dimensions of Human Consciousness. Includes our *Surface* waking consciousness; *Liminal* consciousness of our feelings, emotions, energy, and aspirations; and *Bedrock* consciousness of intuitions and dreams that link us to *Universal Consciousness.* The dimensions are expressions of the essential "withoutness" (outside) and "withinness" (inside) of everything described by Teilhard de Chardin.

Ego. the part of the human psyche that mediates between the dimensions of consciousness that ascertains what is real and establishes a sense of personal identity.

Emergence. Characterizes the biodiversity of the earth, human consciousness, the emotions, and the biochemical processes that cannot be understood in terms of simple laws. The emergent behavior and phenomena are unpredictable and irreducible because the interaction of the parts can produce an infinite number of patterns.

Empiricism. A Way of Knowing that represents objective reality and truth as verified by evidence.

Entanglement. Particles that have once interacted become "entangled" and thereafter correlate with one another's internal states (like spin) instantly, regardless of the spatial or temporal distances the two particles have since traveled. Entangled particles form an indivisible whole and cannot be treated as if they were separate from one another (from Kripal, 100).

Epistemology. The academic field that studies *how we know* reality based on our five senses and our intuition.

Fields of Consciousness. Wavy fields of quantum energy and information that penetrate the whole of the Universe. The fields are entangled and interact with the energy fields of our world in a manifestation of Consciousness that interacts with the dimensions of our human consciousness.

Holism. A focus on whole systems rather than the parts. Self-organizing systems of endless levels of complexity can be best understood by focusing on the whole instead of breaking components down into their smallest parts. Parts can only be understood when we view them in relation to the whole.

Holos. The collective intelligence of all humans combined with the collective behavior of all machines, plus the intelligence of nature and whatever behavior emerges from this whole in the Surface dimension of consciousness.

Human consciousness. Our waking awareness of linking the moments, events, images, and ideas in life to create patterns that are our reality. These patterns come and go and combine and recombine, sometimes unpredictably. When asleep, we engage Consciousness in our *Bedrock consciousness.*

Imaginal figures. "Inner" figures, unique to a particular person, or representations of "outer" figures that can be investigated through dream figures, reverie, and active imagination.

Imaginal reality. A dynamic and real place of experience, inhabited by multivocal, multivalent beings, including interior figures and images that are neither fully matter nor fully spirit.

Insight. A *Way of Knowing* that combines our intuitive way of perceiving things and our ability to make meaning through our personal experience, including our ability to sense "something more" from Consciousness that is not able to be described by our senses.

Large Hadron Collider (LHC). The world's largest and highest-energy particle collider in a tunnel beneath the France–Switzerland border. Physicists hope that the LHC will find a grand force that underlies everything. Consciousness is this underlying and unifying force that the scientists are looking for.

Liminal dimension of consciousness. The turbulent, thermodynamic bodily liquids and gases; the emotions, feelings, and desires; and the spiritual longings that propel action at the Surface dimension of human consciousness.

Mystic. A spiritual seeker who attains insights beyond the intellect through expansion of consciousness of the world around them and through contact with a divine or higher consciousness.

Mystical experience. A state of being when our Surface consciousness merges with Universal Consciousness, usually creating feelings of bliss, awe, unconditional love, and interconnectedness with everything.

Near-death experiences (NDEs). Complex experiential episodes that occur in association with death or the perception that death is impending. They are intensely vivid and often life-transforming. Many occur with trauma, ceasing of brain activity, deep general anesthesia, or cardiac arrest in which no awareness or sensory experiences should be possible according to the prevailing views in neuroscience.

Non-duality. Also called nondualism. Primarily refers to a state of humanconsciousness in which the dichotomy of "I" and "other" is transcended.

Non-local. Human consciousness is not confined to specific points in space, such as brains and bodies, or specific moments in time, such as the present.

Noosphere. The sphere of human consciousness that influences the evolution of the biosphere. Pierre Teilhard de Chardin said as humanity became more self-reflective and able to appreciate its place in space and time, it would evolve the evolution of the noosphere by great leaps instead of a slow climb.

Numinous. Denotes "arousing spiritual or religious emotion; mysterious or awe-inspiring." Theologian and philosopher Rudolf Otto popularized the term in his influential 1917 book, *The Idea of the Holy*.

Omega Point. The "point" in creation, theorized Pierre Teilhard de Chardin, that draws (or lures) our consciousness to a spiritual level.

Ontology. The academic field of *descriptions of reality* that is ultimately based on belief and faith that what we *think* we know is true. In contrast, epistemology is the academic field about *how* we know reality based on our five senses and our intuition.

Perennial Wisdom. The central idea is that ultimate reality is one, timeless, and universal, and that the different religions are but different languages expressing that one Truth, often symbolized by the uncolored light and the many colors of the spectrum that are made visible when the uncolored light is refracted by a prism.

Physicalism. The metaphysical assertion that everything is physical, that there is nothing superior to the physical.

Portals to Consciousness. The many ways to enter the mystical domain and access Universal Consciousness.

Praxis. A *Way of Knowing* through acting on our understanding and inner sensations—who and how we are and why we are here. In *Praxis* we enact, practice, and embody a theory or lesson. Ideas and skills are engaged, applied, and realized.

Presence. An awareness of the larger whole, leading to actions that can help to shape our future by sensing the unfolding whole within each of us and within the present situation, and acting in service of it.

Prism. A metaphor of human consciousness. When the light of Universal Consciousness enters the prism of our human consciousness, it casts colorful and diverse light that enlightens our worldview. Consciousness is continually reframing, reimagining, and reforming our consciousness of the physical world, including all of our human constructions.

Quantum biology. Describes how life's roots reach down from the cells of living things on the surface through the turbulent middle thermodynamic layer to penetrate the quantum bedrock. This allows life to harness the strange quantum reality to allow enzymes to speed up chemical reactions. The quantum biology model of life at the edge of quantum reality provides a strong metaphor for all aspects of our lives, including our physical being, our conscious awareness, and our sense of a transcendent spirit.

Quark. A type of elementary particle that is a fundamental constituent of matter. Quarks combine to form protons and neutrons, the components of atomic nuclei.

Reality. A framework in which people organize their beliefs around axioms that are contained in the worldviews they have inherited.

Reflexive Monism. A theory of reality by Max Velmans that integrates realism and idealism, dualism and monism, ordinary experience and mystical experience, and the mind and the brain.

Self. Refers both to the larger "Self," which is empowered and not restricted to the demands of the ego, and to our smaller "self," which is focused on survival and security. The larger Self (also called the True Self) is driven by a need for self-actualization, serving others, and doing worthwhile things. We have the capacity to transcend our material and social needs and values to achieve a larger Self.

Shadow. In analytical psychology, the shadow is an unconscious aspect of the personality that the conscious ego has suppressed or is an aspect of the personality that is unknown.

Surface Dimension of consciousness. The macro, everyday world of physical objects, people, nature, and the universe where physical objects and behavior can be observed, measured, and predicted (at least with known probabilities).

Synchronicity. A strong metaphor for describing how disparate elements without apparent connection are brought together or juxtaposed in a manner that tends to shock or surprise the mind, rendering it open to new possibilities. The recognition of synchronicity is often linked to the presence of Universal Consciousness.

Thin Place. A Celtic Christian term for locales and instances where the walls and boundaries between dimensions of consciousness are dissolved.

Transcendent function. A mediating force identified by Carl Jung that holds a creative tension between what is happening in Surface consciousness, and the unknown and unpredictable possibilities in Bedrock consciousness, enabling transformation.

Transpersonal. A state of consciousness beyond the limits of personal identity, and beyond the space and time of our three-dimensional world.

Transrational reality. Refers to the nonpersonal, nonrational phenomena such as dreams that are not explainable by standard cause-and-effect logical structures.

True Self, False Self. Psychological concepts originally introduced into psychoanalysis in 1960 by Donald Winnicott to describe a sense of self based on spontaneous authentic experience, and a feeling of being alive and having a real self.

Tunneling. The quantum phenomenon of particles in an atom passing through barriers while in a wave state. Big objects made up of trillions of atoms cannot behave in a coherent, wave-like fashion. However, the enzymes in living cells make tunneling possible.

Universal Consciousness, Universal Mind, or Cosmic Consciousness. A metaphysical concept about an underlying essence of all being and becoming in the universe. In experiencing Universal Consciousness, there is no experience of body or thoughts; there is a connection with everything in a beautiful harmony of constant transformation. Buddhists say there is no self because a self cannot be experienced in Universal Consciousness.

Ways of Knowing. Refers to representing reality and truth from multiple sources, including *Insight* (subjective reality), *Authority* (normative reality), *Empiricism* (objective reality), and *Praxis* (practical reality). The interaction of these multiple sources yields deeper levels of knowledge.

Wholeness. The quality of being or feeling complete and not fragmented. The wholeness we experience in health, peace, welfare, rest, harmony, joy, etc., is always in transition. The *Wholeness Model* provides a way to regain a new or renewed whole state by experiencing Universal Consciousness and finding deeper meaning and unconditional love.

Wholeness Model (Figure 10). Based on the quantum biology depiction of life, is a method to facilitate connecting and integrating human dimensions of consciousness—Surface, Liminal and Bedrock—and to connect to Universal Consciousness.

Appendix A
My Extended Family

On June 20, 2021, while editing this book, I had this dream:

> I need to dedicate the book to the spirit of my pets throughout my
> life with pictures.

As I wrote down the dream, the imaginal figures of several pets felt
very present.

My first and only childhood pet was "Queenie," a red Chow-Chow
I had while living in Hazel Park, Michigan, from birth to sixth grade. My
parents, Arne and Helga, and I then moved to a farm in Jackson, Minnesota. From seventh grade until I left for college, I had three pets: "Byrd,"
a parakeet; "Spike," a collie, and "Sis," a Duroc pig that I took to the county
fair. (The only explanation I have for her name is that I am an only child.)

After marrying Judith and living with our four children, our pets
were: "Oliver," an orange cat; "Schnoodle," a Schnauzer/Poodle; "Suzie," an
English sheepdog; "Betsy," a pedigreed Welsh Corgi we bought in England
during a sabbatical, and her son "William."

In 1990, my children gave me a Shar-pei puppy we named "Prunella"
(Pru) for her many wrinkles. She became a mainstay during our years in
Maryland and Minnesota. Her death in 2004 was traumatic. Her spirit was
with us for years. Versions of her name became our computer passwords
(which I now have to change after this disclosure).

Pru's presence was so strong that we did not want another pet. Perhaps because of the COVID-19 isolation and our settled life in Tennessee, in early 2021 we had the emotional space for another pet. We found
Trixie, a calico cat, in an animal shelter in Crossville Tennessee. She has
since become an integral part of the family. She has four cat towers to help

her look out windows at many squirrels and birds. We pondered getting a companion for Trixie because she exhausts us with wanting to play, but we only occasionally babysit our daughter's pug named "Beatrice."

As I recorded the dream that spurred me to acknowledge these pets, I felt the presence of the consciousness of each pet. Trixie, of course, came over to see what I was doing and then promptly fell asleep beside me in Judith's chair.

There is more and more research about the consciousness of mammals, reptiles, and even insects that could be a future book. As I meditated on this, images formed of my time with Spike and Prunella, but I only had a one-way communication.

About the Author

Ed Olson was a survey research director for National Analysts, Inc., and senior associate at the Institute for the Advancement of Medical Communication. He then was appointed as professor of information service at the University of Maryland, College Park, and then professor of management at Baldwin-Wallace College. He ended his full-time professional career as an organization development and diversity consultant to many companies and government agencies.

He is a member of the NTL Institute of Applied Behavioral Science and a National Certified Counselor. Currently he teaches an online MBA course for the University of Maryland, Global Campus (UMGC), and leads workshops for churches and the Chautauqua Institution. He applies complexity, consciousness, and quantum theories to integrating science, spirituality, and religion in order to influence the prevailing materialist worldview.

Ed has a BA in Philosophy (St. Olaf College); MS in Pastoral Counseling (Loyola College); MA and PhD in Government (American University); and is a graduate of the Science for Ministry Program, Princeton Theological Seminary.

He is the author of *And God Created Wholeness: A Spirituality of Catholicity* (2018, Orbis Books); *Finding Reality: Four Ways of Knowing* (2014, Archway Publications); *Keep the Bathwater: Emergence of the Sacred in Science and Religion* (2009, Island Sound Press); *Facilitating Organization Change: Lessons from Complexity Science* (2001, Jossey-Bass/Wiley), and numerous papers and presentations at national and international conferences.

Ed is married 62 years to Judith. They live in Uplands Village, Pleasant Hill, Tennessee, and have four children (James, Eric, Loren, and Amy) and eight grandchildren (Preston, Arne, Arlo, Greta, Zeida, Tuesday, Cisco, and Clover).

His website, Wholeness Consciousness (wholenessconsciousness .com), offers fresh content from diverse perspectives to keep this conversation going. Hopefully, readers will contribute their own ideas for moving us, individually and collectively, toward the Wholeness we need to respond to our existential crises.

BIBLIOGRAPHY

Aizenstat, Stephen. "Dream Tending, Techniques for Uncovering the Hidden Intelligence of Your Dreams." *Spring Journal* (2011).

Alex, Briget. "The Anthropocene's Ancient Origins." *Discover Magazine* (July/August 2021) 62–65.

Alexander, Eben, and Karen Newell. *Explore the Near-Death Experience Through Science, Spirituality & Sound.* Modules 3, 5, 6. IMH Lab, 2020.

———. *Living in a Mindful Universe: A Neurosurgeon's Journey into the Heart of Consciousness.* Rodale: 2017.

Anthony, Mark. *Evidence of Eternity: Communicating with Spirits for Proof of the Afterlife.* Llewellyn, 2015.

Appelbaum, Binyamin. "Blaming Milton Friedman." *New York Times* (September 19, 2020) A: 22.

Artress, Lauren. *Walking a Sacred Path: Rediscovering the Labyrinth as a Spiritual Practice.* New York: Riverhead, 2006.

Bache, Christopher M. "Teaching in the New Paradigm." 2016. https://www.academia.edu/4077612/Teaching-in-the-New-Paradigm.

Barnett, Lincoln. *The Universe and Dr. Einstein.* 2nd rev. ed. New York: Bantam, 1957.

Barrett, Lisa Feldman. *Seven and a Half Lessons About the Brain.* New York: Houghton-Mifflin: 2020.

Bass, Diane Butler. "Awakening Now?" *The Cottage* (August 17, 2020).

Bates, Charles. *Pigs Eat Wolves: Going into Partnership With Your Dark Side.* 2nd ed. St. Paul, MN: Yes International, 2001.

Beichler, James E. "Consciousness Manifesto: Physical Origins of Consciousness Through Evolution and Revolution." *WISE Journal*, SSE/ASCSI (2017).

———. "The Consciousness Revolution in Science: The Inner Workings of the Primal Cosmic Mish-Mash Which Yields Our Senses of Spirit, Consciousness and Our Interpretations of Nature/Physics." *ASCSI/SFF Conference* (October 6, 2018).

Beitman, Bernard D. *Connecting with Coincidence: The New Science for Using Synchronicity and Serendipity in Your Life.* Health Communications Inc., 2016.

Bell, Rob. *Love Wins: A Book About Heaven, Hell, and the Fate of Every Person Who Ever Lived.* HarperOne, 2012.

Benner, David G. "Perfection and the Harmonics of Wholeness." *Oneing*, Vol. 4, No. 1, CAC (2016) 62–63.

Bernstein, Gabrielle. *Super Attractor.* Hay House, 2021.

Bibliography

Bernstein, Jerome S. *Living in the Borderland: Healing the Split Between Psyche and Nature.* Routledge, 2005. www.borderlanders.com.

Bhadra, Narayan Kumar. "The Complex Quantum-State of Consciousness." *IOSR Journal of Biotechnology and Biochemistry.* Vol. 5, Issue 1 (Jan.–Feb. 2019) 58–93.

Blake, Anthony. *A Gymnasium of Beliefs.* DuVersity, 2009.

Bohm, David. *Wholeness and Implicate Order.* 175. London: Routledge & Kegan Paul, 1980.

Boje, David M., and Ken Baskin. *Dance to the Music of Story: Understanding Human Behavior Through the Integration of Storytelling and Complexity Thinking.* Litchfield Park, Arizona: Emergent, 2010.

Bondarev, Vladimir. *The New Science of Consciousness.* ASIN: B08N9GLMRH, 2020.

Borg, Marcus. *The Heart of Christianity.* San Francisco: Harper, 2003.

Borowski, Susan. "Quantum Mechanics and the Consciousness Connection." *AAAS* (July 16, 2010). https://www.aaas.org/quantum-mechanics-and-consciousness-connection.

Bouie, Jamelle. "Our Illusions." *New York Times* (Nov. 1, 2020) SR:11.

Bourgeault, Cynthia. *Eye of the Heart: A Spiritual Journey into the Imaginal Realm.* Boulder, CO: Shambhala, 2020.

———. *The Wisdom Jesus: Transforming Heart and Mind—A New Perspective on Christ and His Message.* Boulder, CO: Shambhala, 2008.

Brooks, David. "The Floor of Decency." *New York Times* (October 28, 2020).

———. "The National Humiliation We Need." *New York Times* (July 3, 2020) A23.

———. "Nine Nonobvious Ways to Have Deeper Conversations: The Art of Making Connection Even in a Time of Dislocation." *New York Times* (November 19, 2020) A29.

———. "This is How Wokeness Ends." *New York Times* (May 14, 2021) A22.

———. "What the Voters Are Trying to Tell Us." *New York Times* (November 6, 2020) A19.

Brooks, Michael. "Is the Universe Conscious?" *New Scientist* (April 29, 2020).

Bulkeley, Kelly. *Dreaming In the World's Religions: A Comparative Survey.* New York: New York University Press, 2008.

Bush, Nancy Evans, and Bruce Greyson. "Distressing Near-Death Experiences." *Missouri Medicine* (December 2014).

Cannato, Judy. *Fields of Compassion: How the New Cosmology is Transforming Spiritual Life.* Notre Dame, IN: Sorin, 2010.

———. *Radical Amazement.* Notre Dame, IN: Sorin, 2006.

Carroll, Robert Todd. "Cellular Memory." 2017. http://skepdic.com/cellular.html.

Chalmers, D. J.. "Consciousness and Its Place in Nature." In *Philosophy of Mind: Classical and Contemporary Readings.* UK: Oxford University Press, 2002.

Chopra, Deepak. *The Third Jesus: The Christ We Cannot Ignore.* New York: Harmony, 2008.

———. "Is the Afterlife a Non-Question? (Let's Hope Not)." *Journal of Consciousness Exploration & Research.* Vol. 7, Issue 11 (December 2016) 1235–1239.

Chopra, Deepak and Menas Kafatos. *You Are the Universe: Discovering Your Cosmic Self and Why It Matters.* New York: Harmony, 2017.

Clayton, Philip. *Transforming Christian Theology for Church and Society.* Minneapolis, MN: Fortress, 2010.

Cohen, Andrew. "The Evolution of Enlightenment." *Spanda* (2012).

Coleman, Flynn. *A Human Algorithm: How Artificial Intelligence is Redefining Who We Are.* Berkeley, CA: Counterpoint, 2019.

Corbett, Lionel. *Psyche and the Sacred: Spirituality Beyond* Religion. New Orleans: Spring Journal Books, 2012.

Cox, Trevor J., et al. "Using Scale Modelling to Assess the Prehistoric Acoustics of Stonehenge." *Journal of Archaeological Science.* Vol. 122 (October 2020).

Curry, Oliver Scott, et al. "Is It Good to Cooperate? Testing the Theory of Morality-as-Cooperation in 60 Societies." *Current Anthropology* (2019).

Delio, Ilia. *Birth of a Dancing Star: My Journey from a Cradle Catholic to a Christian Cyborg.* Maryknoll, NY: Orbis, 2019.

———. *Hours of the Universe: Reflections on God, Science, and the Human Journey.* Maryknoll, NY: Orbis, 2021.

———. *A Hunger for Wholeness: Soul, Space, and Transcendence.* Paulist Press, Kindle Edition, 2018.

———. *Making All Things New: Catholicity, Cosmos, and Consciousness.* Maryknoll, NY: Orbis, 2015.

———. *Re-Enchanting the Earth: Why AI Needs* Religion. Maryknoll, NY: Orbis, 2020.

———. *The Unbearable Wholeness of Being: God, Evolution, and the Power of Love.* Maryknoll, NY: Orbis, 2013.

Deloria, Vine. *God is Red: A Native View of Religion.* Fulcrum, 2002.

Dewey, Art. *The Fourth R.* 33:5 (Sept.–Oct. 2020) 2.

Di Biase, Francisco. "The Unified of Consciousness." dibiase@terra.com.br.

Dossey, Larry. *One Mind: How Our Individual Mind Is Part of a Greater Consciousness and Why It Matters.* Carlsbad, CA: Hayhouse Inc., 2013.

Eddington, Arthur. *The Nature of the Physical World.* New York: Macmillan, 1929.

Einstein, Albert. "The Merging of the Spirit and Science." In *The Universe and Dr. Einstein.* Lincoln Barnett, 2nd rev. ed. New York: Bantam, 1957.

Einstein, Albert, and George Bernard Shaw. *Einstein on Cosmic Religion and Other Opinions and Aphorisms.* Dover Publications: Dover edition, 2009.

Eisen, Jeffrey. *The Omnius Manifesto.* 2011. Essay at http://drjeffreisen.com.

Epstein, Robert. "The Empty Brain." *Aeon* (June 5, 2018).

Estes, Clarissa Pinkola. "Do Not Lose Heart, We Were Made for These Times." *moonmagazine.org* (March 13, 2020).

Eurich, Tasha. "What Self-Awareness Really Is (and How to Cultivate It)." *Harvard Business Review* (January 4, 2018).

Finley, James. *Thomas Merton's Path to the Palace of Nowhere.* Audiobook. Sounds True, 2004.

Fisher, Max. "Belonging is Stronger than Facts: The Age of Misinformation." *New York Times* (May 7, 2021).

Fox, Matthew. *Meister Eckhart: A Mystic Warrior for our Times.* Novato, CA: New World Library, 2014.

———. *Julian of Norwich: Wisdom in a Time of Pandemic–and Beyond.* Bloomington, IN: iUniverse, 2020.

Fredriksson, Ingrid, ed. *The Mysteries of Consciousness: Essays on Spacetime, Evolution and Well-Being.* Forthcoming.

Global Consciousness Project. Institute of Noetic Sciences, http://noosphere.princeton.edu/homepage.html.

Global Trends Report. National Intelligence Council, 2021.

Gober, Mark. *An End to Upside Down Living: Reorienting Our Consciousness to Live Better and Save the Human Species.* Cardiff-by-the-Sea, CA: Waterside Press, 2020.

———. *An End to Upside Down Thinking: Dispelling the Myth that the Brain Produces Consciousness, and the Implications for Everyday Life.* Cardiff-by-the-Sea, CA: Waterside, 2018.

Goff, Philip. *Galileo's Error: Foundations for a New Science of Consciousness.* New York: Pantheon, 2019.

Greyson, Bruce. *After: A Doctor Explores What Near-Death Experiences Reveal about Life and Beyond.* St. Martin's Essentials, 2021.

Gupta, Abhishek, and Victoria Heath. "A.I. Ethics Groups Repeating One of Society's Mistakes." *MIT Technology Review* (September 16, 2020).

Hameroff, Stuart, and Deepak Chopra. "The Quantum Soul: A Scientific Hypothesis." In *Exploring Frontiers of the Mind–Brain Relationship, Mindfulness in Behavioral Health.* Edited by A. Moreira-Almeida, and F. S. Santos. Springer Science+Business Media, 2012.

Hancox, Diane. "Dreams Are the Royal Road to the Unconscious." In *Soul Reflections: Living a More Conscious and Meaningful Life.* Downloaded September 8, 2011.

Hansen, Rick. *Neurodharma: New Science, Ancient Wisdom, and Seven Practices of the Highest Happiness.* New York: Harmony, 2020.

Harari, Yuval Noah. *21 Lessons for the 21st Century.* New York: Random House, 2018.

———. *Homo Deus: A Brief History of Tomorrow.* New York: Harper, 2017.

Hardy, Chris H. "Nonlocal Consciousness in the Universe." *Journal of Nonlocality: Special Issue on Psi and Nonlocal Mind* (2017).

Harrell, Mary. *Imaginal Figures in Everyday Life: Stories From the World Between Matter and Mind.* Asheville, NC: InnerQuest, 2015.

Harvey, Andrew, and Carolyn Baker. *Radical Regeneration: Birthing the New Human in the Age of Extinction.* iUniverse, 2020.

Hebert, Cara. "Am I a Mystic? 10 Telltale Signs of Mystics." *Gaia* (February 6, 2020). https://www.gaia.com/article/am-i-a-mystic-10-signs.

Herrmann, Stephen. *William James and C.G. Jung: Doorways to the Self.* Oberlin, Ohio: Analytical Psychology, 2020.

Hofstadter, Douglas. *I Am a Strange Loop.* New York: Basic, 2007.

Hollis, James. *Finding Meaning in the Second Half of Life: How to Finally, Really Grow Up.* New York: Gotham, 2005.

Holmes, Barbara A. *Race and the Cosmos.* 2nd ed. Albuquerque, NM: CAC, 2020.

Homans, Peter. *Jung in Context: Modernity and the Making of a Psychology.* Chicago: University of Chicago, 1979.

Hood, R.W. "The Construction and Preliminary Validation of a Measure of Reported Mystical Experience." *Journal for the Scientific Study of Religion.* 14:1 (1975) 29.

Hu, Huping, and Maosin Wu, eds. "The Original Principle & Cosmic Perspective of Consciousness." *Journal of Consciousness Exploration & Research.* 10:2 (March 2019).

Hunt, Tam. "Could Consciousness All Come Down to the Way Things Vibrate?" *The Conversation.* (November 9, 2018).

Huxley, Aldous. *The Doors of Perception.* New York: Perennial Library, 1954/1991.

Jacobs, Andrew. "The Psychedelic Revolution Is Coming. Psychiatry May Never Be the Same." *New York Times* (May 11, 2021).

James, William. *Human Immortality: Two Supposed Objections to the Doctrine* (The Ingersoll Lectureship). New York: Houghton, Mifflin, 1898.

Johnston, Margaret Placentra. *Overcoming Spiritual Myopia: A View Toward Peace Among the Religions.* 2018.

Jung, Carl G. "The Meaning of Psychology for Modern Man." CW 10: Civilization in Transition (1933) 304.

Jung, Carl G., *Modern Man in Search of a Soul.* NY: Harcourt Brace, 1955.

———. *On the Psychology of the Unconscious.* 1917.

Kafatos, Menas C. "Bridging the Perceived Gap Between Science and Metaphysics: The Primacy of Consciousness and Experience." In *Is Consciousness Primary?* Vol.1 Postmaterialist Sciences Series. Edited by Steven A. Schwartz et al. Battleground, WA: Academy for the Advancement of Postmaterialist Sciences, 2020.

Kafatos, Menas, and Robert Nadeau. *The Conscious Universe.* New York: Springer, 1990.

Kastrup, Bernardo. *Decoding Jung's Metaphysics: The Archetypal Semantics of an Experiential Universe.* Hampshire, England: Iff Books, 2021.

———. *More Than Allegory: On Religious Myth, Truth and Belie.* Hampshire, England: Iff Books, 2016.

———. "Physics is Pointing Inexorably to Mind." *Scientific American* (March 25, 2019).

———. *Why Materialism Is Baloney: How True Skeptics Know There Is No Death and Fathom Answers to Life, the Universe, and Everything.* Hampshire, England: Iff Books, 2014.

Kastrup, Bernardo, et al. "Could Multiple Personality Disorder Explain Life, the Universe and Everything?" *Scientific American* (2018).

Kauffman, Stuart A. *Reinventing the Sacred: A New View of Science, Reason, and Religion.* New York: Basic, 2008.

Kaufman, Scott Barry. "What Would Happen If Everyone Truly Believed Everything Is One?" *Scientific American* (October 8, 2018).

Kaur, Valarie. *See No Stranger: A Memoir and Manifesto of Revolutionary Love.* One World: 2020.

Kearny, Richard. *Anatheism.* New York: Columbia University Press, 2011.

Kellerer, Catherine. *Cloud of the Impossible.* New York: Columbia University Press, 2015.

Kelly, Edward, and P. Marshall, eds. *Consciousness Unbound.* Lanham, MD: Rowman and Littlefield, 2020.

Kelly, Edward, and Emily Williams Kelly. *Irreducible Mind: Toward a Psychology for the 21st Century.* Rowman and Littlefield, 2009.

Kornfield, Jack. "Open Hearts, Open Minds." In *The New Possible: Visions of Our World Beyond Crisis.* Edited by Philip Clayton et al. Eugene, OR: Cascade (2021) 201–209.

Korten, David C. "Telling a New Story." In *The New Possible: Visions of Our World Beyond Crisis.* Edited by Philip Clayton et al. Eugene, Oregon: Cascade (2021) 259–267.

Kourie, Celia. "Weaving Colorful Threads: A Tapestry of Spirituality and Mysticism." *HTS Theological Studies* 71:1 (2015) 7.

Kripal, Jeffrey J. *The Flip: Epiphanies of Mind and the Future of Knowledge.* New York: Bellevue Literary, 2019.

Laloux, Frederic, and Ken Wilber. *Reinventing Organizations: A Guide to Creating Organizations Inspired by the Next Stage in Human Consciousness.* 2014.

Laszlo, Ervin. *New Science for a New World: The Rise of the Akasha Paradigm.* 2013.

———. *Reconnecting to the Source: The New Science of Spiritual Experience, How It Can Change You, and How It Can Transform the World.* New York: St. Martin Essentials, 2020.

————. *What is Reality? The New Map of Cosmos and Consciousness.* New York: Select, 2016.

Lawson, Finley. "Complete in Manhood—Understanding Christ's Humanity in Light of Quantum Holism." Paper presented at European Conference of Science and Theology XVI, Lodz, Poland, 2016.

Lebron, Chris. "White America Wants Me to Conform. I Won't Do It." *New York Times* (June 16, 2020).

Levy, Paul. *The Quantum Revelation: A Radical Synthesis of Science and Spirituality.* New York: Select, 2018.

Lindhard, Tina. "Consciousness from the Outside-In and Inside-Out Perspective." *Journal of Consciousness Explorations & Research.* Vol. 10, Issue 3 (April 2019).

————. "The Theory of Six Main Levels of Consciousness: A Study of the Third Level." *Journal of Consciousness, Exploration and Research.* 9:1 (January 2018).

Lomas, Tim. *Translating Happiness: A Cross-Cultural Lexicon of Well-Being.* Boston: MIT Press, 2018.

Lovelock, James E. "A Physical Basis for Life Detection Experiments." *Nature* (1965).

Manjoo, Farhad. "There Is Only One Existential Threat. Let's Talk About It: Our Political Culture Isn't Ready to Deal with Climate Change." *New York Times* (October 28, 2020).

Marshall, Paul. *Mystical Encounters with the Natural World.* Oxford: Oxford University Press, 2005.

Masters, Robert A. *The Anatomy of Intuition: The Everyday Transmission of Nonconceptual Knowingness.* https://www.robertmasters.com/writings/the-anatomy-of-intuition/

Mattson, Jill. *The Lost Waves of Time: The Untold Story of How Music Shaped Our World.* Oil City, PA: Wings of Light, 2015.

McFadden, Johnjoe, and Jim Al-Khalili. *Life on the Edge: The Coming of Age of Quantum Biology.* New York: Crown, 2014.

Medlock, Ben. "The Body is the Missing Link for Truly Intelligent Machines." *Aeon* (March 14, 2017).

Meijer, Dirk K.F., and Hans J. H. Geesink. "Consciousness in the Universe is Scale Invariant and Implies an Event Horizon of the Human Brain." *NeuroQuantology* 15:3 (September 2017) 41–79.

Meijer, Dirk K.F. "Universal Consciousness: Collective Evidence on the Basis of Current Physics and Philosophy." https://www.researchgate.net/profile/Dirk_Meijer4.

Meijer, Dirk K.F., et al. "Consciousness in the Universe, Part 3." *Quantum Biosystems,* Vol. 11, No. 1 (2020).

Merton, Thomas. *Conjectures of a Guilty Bystander.* Doubleday & Company, 1965.

————. *New Seeds of Contemplation.* New Directions, 1961.

Meyers, Robin R. "If There Is No Theistic God Does Prayer Even Make Sense?" ProgressiveChristianity.org, May 28, 2021.

————. *Saving God from Religion.* Contingent, 2020.

Miller–Idriss, Cynthia. *Hate in the Homeland: The New Global Far Right.* Princeton, NJ: Princeton University Press, 2020.

Mitchell, Stephen. *The Enlightened Mind.* Harper, 1993.

Moreira-Almeida, A., and F.S. Santos, eds. *Exploring Frontiers of the Mind – Brain Relationship, Mindfulness in Behavioral Health.* Springer Science+Business Media, 2012.

Moss, Robert. *Growing Big Dreams: Manifesting Your Heart Desires Through 12 Secrets of the Imagination*. Novato, CA: New World Library, 2020.

Murray, Don. *The Bible Beyond Religion: Witness to the Evolution of Consciousness*. Las Vegas, NV: Tellwell Talent, 2021.

Neale, Lex. "Integral Relativity of Awareness and Energy – the Continuum of Consciousness, Energy, Mind, and Matter." *NeuroQuantology* 16:8 (August 2018) 173.

Olson, Edwin E. *And God Created Wholeness: A Spirituality of Catholicity*. Maryknoll, NY: Orbis, 2018.

————. *Finding Reality: Four Ways of Knowing*. Bloomington, IN: Archway, 2014.

————. *Keep the Bathwater: Emergence of the Sacred in Science and Religion*. Estero, FL: Island Sound, 2009.

Olson, Edwin E., and John D. Crowell. "Self-Creating and Quantum Theories of Human Spirituality: Developing a Unifying Narrative of Science and Religion." Paper presented at the Conference of the European Society for the Study of Science and Theology, Lodz, Poland, 2016.

Ó Murchú, Diarmuid. *Quantum Theology: Spiritual Implications of the New Physics* rev. ed. Crossroad, 2004.

Ord, Toby. *The Precipice: Existential Risk and the Future of Humanity*. Hachette, 2020.

Oschman, J. L., and N. H. Oschman. "The Heart as a Bi-directional Scalar Field Antenna." *Journal of Vortex Science and Technology*. 2 (2015) 121.

Palmer, Parker. *A Hidden Wholeness: The Journey Toward an Undivided Life*. San Francisco: Jossey-Bass, 2009.

Patton, Terry. *A New Republic of the Heart: An Ethos for Revolutionaries*. Berkeley, CA: North Atlantic, 2018.

Pereira, Jr., Alfredo, et al. "Consciousness and Cosmos: Building an Ontological Framework." *Journal of Consciousness Studies*. 25:3–4 (2018) 181–205.

Pereira, Contzen, and J. Shashi Kiran Reddy. "The Manifestation of Consciousness: Beyond & Within from Fundamental to Ubiquity." *Journal of Consciousness Exploration & Research*. Vol. 8:1 (January 2017) 51–55.

Phillips, Jan. *No Ordinary Time: The Rise of Spiritual Intelligence and Evolutionary Christianity*. San Diego, CA: Livingkindness Foundation, 2011.

Piaget, Jean. *A Child's Conception of Space*. Norton Edition, 1967.

Planck, Max. Interview, *The Observer* (January 25, 1931).

Pollan, Michael. "In Search of a Politics of Resilience: On the Field and in the Mind." In *The New Possible: Visions of Our World Beyond Crisis*. Edited by Philip Clayton et al. Eugene, OR: Cascade, 2021, 63–70.

Ponte, Diogo, et al. "Carl Gustav Jung, Quantum Physics and the Spiritual Mind: A Mystical Vision of the Twenty-First Century." *Behavioral Sciences*. Vol. 3 (2013) 601–18.

Pramuk, Christopher. In *Sophia: the Hidden Christ of Thomas Merton*. Collegeville, MN: Liturgical, 2009.

Radin, Dean R. *Real Magic: Ancient Wisdom, Modern Science, and a Guide to the Secret Power of the Universe*. New York: Harmony, 2018.

Raymo, Chet. *When God is Gone, Everything is Holy*. New York: Soren, 2008.

Renesch, John. "Conscious Leadership Coaching." *Coaching Psychology International*. 10:2 (Summer 2017).

Reps, Paul, and Nyogen Senzaki, compilers. *Zen Flesh, Zen Bones: A Collection of Zen and Pre-Zen Writings*. Tuttle, 1998.

Robinson, John. *Mystical Activism: Transforming a World in Crisis*. Winchester, UK: Changemaker, 2020. www.johnrobinson.org.

Robinson, John A.T. *Honest to God*. SCM Classic, 2011.

Robson, David. "The 'Untranslatable' Emotions You Never Knew You Had." *BBC Future*, 2020.

Rohr, Richard. *Adam's Return: The Five Promises of Male Initiation*. The Crossroad Publishing Company: 2004.

———. *Falling Upward: A Spirituality for the Two Halves of Life*. San Francisco: Jossey-Bass: 2011.

———. *Immortal Diamond: The Search for Our True Self*. San Francisco: Jossey-Bass, 2013.

———. *Things Hidden: Scripture as Spirituality*. Cincinnati, OH: St. Anthony Messenger, 2007.

———. *True Self/False Self*. Disc 2. Franciscan Media, 2003.

———. *The Universal Christ: How a Forgotten Reality Can Change Everything We See, Hope For, and Believe*. New York: Convergent, 2019.

———. *What Do We Do with Evil? The World, the Flesh, and the Devil*. CAC (2019) 79–81, 83, 85.

———. *What the Mystics Know: Seven Pathways to Your Deeper Self*. The Crossroad Publishing Company, 2015.

———. *The Wisdom Pattern*. Franciscan Media, 2020.

Rosenstein, Justin and the One Project Team. "The Architect of Abundance: A Path to a Democratic Economy." In *The New Possible: Visions of Our World Beyond Crisis*. Edited by Philip Clayton et al. Eugene, OR: Cascade (2021) 33–44.

Russell, Bertrand. "Mind and Matter." 1950. https://russell-j.com/19501110_Mind-Matter.HTM.

Sabbadini, Shantena Augusto. *Pilgrimages To Emptiness: Rethinking Reality through Quantum Physics*. Pari, Italy: Pari, 2017.

Sacks, Jonathan. *The Dignity of Difference: How to Avoid the Clash of Civilizations*. New York: Continuum, 2002.

Sadhguru. *Karma: A Yogi's Guide to Crafting Your Destiny*. New York: Harmony, 2021.

Sala, Luc. *Ritual: The Magical Perspective: Efficacy and the Search for Inner Meaning*. 2014. http://www.lucsala.nl/ritual/1.pdf.

Samuel, Sigal. "Atheists Are Sometimes More Religious than Christians." *The Atlantic* (May 31, 2018).

Savary, Louis M. *Teilhard de Chardin's The Phenomenon of Man Explained*. New York: Paulist 2020.

Schiltz, Marilyn. "Emerging Worldviews: Tools for Transformation for Noetic Leadership." In *Consciousness & Development* 2.0: *An Operating Manual*. Edited by Sahlan, Momo. *Spanda Journal* (2012).

Schneider, Kirk J. "Today's Biggest Threat: The Polarized Mind." *Scientific American* (2020).

Schrodinger, Erwin. *What is Life?* Translated by Verena Schrodinger. Cambridge: Cambridge University Press, reprint edition (2012) 93–95.

Schwartz, Stephan A. "The Transformation—Nonlocal Consciousness Becomes a Fundamental in Our Reality." *Explore*. Elsevier, Inc., 2019.

Schwartz, Steven A., et al. *Is Consciousness Primary?* Vol. 1. Postmaterialist Sciences Series. Battleground, WA: Academy for the Advancement of Postmaterialist Sciences, 2020.

Selbie, Joseph. *The Physics of God: Unifying Quantum Physics, Consciousness, M-Theory, Heaven, Neuroscience, and Transcendence.* Newburyport, MA: New Page, 2018.

Sepie, Amba J. "Listening to the Elders: Earth Consciousness and Ecology." In *Greening the Paranormal: Exploring the Ecology of Extraordinary Experience.* Edited by Jack Hunter. White Crow, 2019.

Sheldrake, Rupert. *Ways to Go Beyond and Why They Work: Seven Spiritual Practices for a Scientific Age.* Rhinebeck, NY: Monkfish, 2019.

Smuts, Jan. *Holism and Evolution.* 1936, Alpha Edition. 2020.

Soelle, Dorothee. *The Silent Cry: Mysticism and Resistance.* Translated by Barbara and Martin Rumscheldt. Minneapolis, MN: Fortress, 2001.

Spira, Rupert. *The Nature of Consciousness: Essays on the Unity of Mind and Matter.* Oakland, CA: New Harbinger, 2017.

Spong, John Shelby. *The Fourth Gospel: Tales of A Jewish Mystic.* New York: HarperCollins, 2013.

Sreenavasan, S. Xie J., et al. "Social Consensus Through the Influence of Dedicated Minorities." *Phys Rev* 22 (July 2011).

Starr, Mirabai. *Wild Mercy: Living the Fierce and Tender Wisdom of the Women Mystics.* Boulder, CO: Sounds True.

Taylor, Mark. *After God.* Chicago: University of Chicago Press, 2007.

Taylor, Steve. *Spiritual Science: Why Science Needs Spirituality to Make Sense of The World.* London: Watkins, 2018.

Teilhard De Chardin, Pierre. *The Divine Milieu.* New York: Harper & Row, 1960.

———. *The Future of Man.* New York: Harper & Row, 1964.

———. *The Heart of Matter.* San Diego, CA: Harcourt, Brace, Jovanovich, 1978.

———. "How I Believe." *Christianity and Evolution.* Translated by René Hague. Orlando, FL: Harcourt, 1969.

———. *Writings in Time of War.* London: William Collins Sons & Co. Ltd., 1968.

Theise, Neil D., and Menas C. Kafatos. "Fundamental Awareness: A Framework for Integrating Science, Philosophy and Metaphysics." *Communicative & Integrative Biology* (2016). DOI: 10.1080/19420889.2016.1155010.

Tillich, Paul. *Systematic Theology.* Vol. 1. Chicago: University of Chicago Press, 1951.

Todd, Peter. *The Individuation of God.* Wilmette, IL: Chiron, 2012.

Tompkins, Peter, and Christopher Bird. *The Secret Life of Plants.* New York: Harper and Row, 1989.

Trinka, Radek, and Radmila Lorencová. *Quantum Anthropology.* Charles University: Karolinum Press, 2016.

Tyler, Jo, "Story Aliveness." In *Dance to the Music of Story: Understanding Human Behavior Through the Integration of Storytelling and Complexity Thinking.* Edited by David M Boje and Ken Baskin. Litchfield Park, AZ: Emergent, 2010.

Underhill, Evelyn. *Practical Wisdom.* Renaissance Classics, 2012. Originally published in 1914.

VandeHei, Jim. "Our New Reality: Three Americas." *Politics & Policy* (January 10, 2021).

Velmans, Max. "Reflective Monism and the Ground of Being." In *Consciousness Unbound.* Edited by E. Kelly and P. Marshall. Lanham, MD: Rowman and Littlefield, 2020.

Vosper, Gretta. *With or Without God: Why the Way We Live is More Important Than What We Believe.* New York: HarperCollins, 2010.

Walsh, Bryan. "America is Losing Its Religion." *Future* (2021).

Wertheim, Margaret. "Lost in Space: The Spiritual Crisis of Newtonian Cosmology." In *Seeing Further: The Story of Science, Discovery, and the Genius of the Royal Society.* Reprint. Edited by Bill Bryson. New York: William Morrow (2011) 81.

Wilber, Ken. *A Theory of Everything.* Boston: Shambhala, 2000.

Wilczek, Frank. *A Beautiful Question: Finding Nature's Deep Design.* New York: Penguin, 2015.

Woollacott, Marjorie Heinz. *Infinite Awareness: The Awakening of a Scientific Mind.* Lanham, MD: Rowman and Littlefield, 2015.

Wright, Jerry R. *Reimagining God and Religion: Essays for the Psychologically Minded.* Asheville, NC: Chiron, 2018.

INDEX

(*education continued*)
  inclusive values, 125–126
  learning from the "other," 126
  sailboat keel metaphor, 123
  Ubuntu, 126
  valuing intuition in, 124–125
  ways of knowing, 124, 156
ego
  definition of, 151
  and dreams, 44, 49–50
  and mysticism, 102
  and challenges, existential crises, 31,
    64, 107, 123, 141
  transforming, 58, 73, 127–128, 142
  turning off, detaching from, 8, 42,
    45, 53, 61, 70, 77, 118
  value of, small self, 83, 86–87, 155
Einstein, Albert, 8, 9, 26, 36, 100n, 124,
  127
Eisen, Jeffrey, 132
emotions, 3, 4, 7, 23, 37, 39, 58, 84,
  151–152
Empiricism, 124
  definition of, 151, 156
  See also ways of knowing
epistemology, 1, 105, 153
  definition of, 151
Epstein, Robert, 13
ESP (extra-sensory perception), 17, 40

Faraday, Michael, 21
Freud, Sigmund, 43

Galileo's error, 12
Geesink, Hans J.H., 16–17
Global Consciousness Project, 22
Global Trends Report, xv
Gnosis, 41
Gober, Mark, 11n, 23, 71, 88n, 115n,
  116, 127n
God, gods, goddesses, xxii, xxiii, 22, 26,
  34, 70, 113, 114–116, 118–119,
  124, 147n
  See also Consciousness and
    Christianity
Google, 96
Gorman, Amanda, 99

government, 121, 133–135, 142, 144
  polarization, 96, 133, 139
Greyson, Bruce, 147–148n
Gut, gut aphorisms, 7, 13, 17, 40, 54,
  142

Hameroff, Stuart, 16
Harari, Yuval, 83, 97n, 110n, 114–115,
  122n, 128, 134, 138
Harrell, Mary, 45n
Harvey, Andrew, 80n, 107
Herrmann, Steven, 30, 34n, 96
Hindu Seers, 71
holism, holos, xii, xiv
  agent of, 99–109, 145
    definition of, 149
  definition of, 152
  Holos project, 105
  surrender of self, 100
  vital spirit, 101
hundredth monkey metaphor, 95
Huxley, Aldous, xxiin, 73

imaginal
  figures, 149, 152
  reality, 77, 152
  realm, 37, 43
  space, 49, 77, 157
ink dot exercise, 26
Insight, 9, 124
  definition of, 152
  See also ways of knowing
Inspector, Yoram, 85
institutions, 71, 92, 93, 103
  accountability in, 106, 109
  business, government, 130–139
  idolatrous, 109
  leaders of, 110
  religious, 112–114, 121
  resources and power of, 109
  transforming, 104, 109–111, 134,
    136, 139, 142
Internet, global consciousness, 87,
  96–97, 122
intuition, 1, 3, 33, 40, 62, 77, 80, 96,
  103, 151,153